THE PORTABLE

SPELL BOOK

QUICK AND SIMPLE
MAGICK YOU CAN DO
ANYTIME, ANYWHERE

ASHLEEN O'GAEA

AVON, MASSACHUSETTS

For He Who Respects and Protects
My Writing Time,
and for my well-nigh witchy friends.

Published by
Adams Media, a division of F+W Media, Inc.
57 Littlefield Street, Avon, MA 02322. U.S.A.
www.adamsmedia.com

ISBN 10: 1-59869-966-0
ISBN 13: 978-1-59869-966-1

Printed in the United States of America.

J I H G F E D C B A

Library of Congress Cataloging-in-Publication Data
is available from the publisher.

This publication is designed to provide accurate and authoritative
information with regard to the subject matter covered. It is sold
with the understanding that the publisher is not engaged in render-
ing legal, accounting, or other professional advice. If legal advice
or other expert assistance is required, the services of a competent
professional person should be sought.

—From a *Declaration of Principles* jointly adopted
by a Committee of the American Bar Association
and a Committee of Publishers and Associations

Many of the designations used by manufacturers and sellers to distinguish their product are claimed as trademarks. Where those
designations appear in this book and Adams Media was aware of a
trademark claim, the designations have been printed with initial
capital letters.

This book is available at quantity discounts for bulk purchases.
For information, please call 1-800-289-0963.

CONTENTS

ACKNOWLEDGMENTS

Many thanks to Andrea Norville for giving me the opportunity to write this book; to my editor, Katie Corcoran Lytle; my agent, Meredith Hays; and to my husband, Jim Law, for taking care of everything else while I write.

INTRODUCTION

At some point or another, whether at work or at home, we've all felt desperate enough to wish for a spell to magickally wipe out our frustrations and take care of our problems. At last, those spells are here!

But wait a minute—you can't go around acting like a character from a video game or fantasy movie! You live a normal life, with friends, neighbors, and coworkers who may think you've gone off the deep end if you stand up and start making elaborate gestures and speaking in verse. Perhaps you're in a jam and need a spell that's quick and to the point. Problem solved! *The Portable Spell Book* is a collection of original charms, chants, brews, and magicks for people looking for "quick fixes" because "normal" solutions aren't doing the trick. It's for folks who want to explore out-of-the-ordinary remedies without calling attention to themselves.

The best way to use this book is to read the first chapter before you move on to the segments about the kind of magick you want to do. It's always good to understand the tools you're working with. Most of the spells and other magicks are quick and easy, but a few require preparation, and some take longer than others. However, once you've read them through, and understand how they work, you'll be able to shorten them and make other modifications so they'll better suit your needs. (By the way, some practitioners spell "magick" without the "k." In this book, we'll use the "k-spelling" as many people do, to distinguish what we're doing from stage magic.)

Of course, you notice home, work, and play overlapping a bit in your life, and they'll overlap a little here, too. As you read the spells and clarifications in each segment, it will probably occur to you that you could use this "at home" spell at work, or that "at play" charm at home. Feel free to mix and match!

This Book Is Not about Wicca!

The religion of Wicca is becoming more popular every day, and it certainly recognizes formalized magick in its Esbats, or full Moon Circles. However, magick isn't Wicca's focus; rather celebration and worship are at its core. Also, while most Wiccans, myself included, *do* work magick, so do lots of other people. All Wiccans are Witches, but not all witches are Wiccan.

Sometimes the "w" in witch(craft) is capitalized, and sometimes it isn't. We capitalize Witchcraft when we're talking about it in a religious context, and when we're not, we don't. Sometimes people use the word Witchcraft as a synonym for Wicca, in which case a capital W is appropriate. When we're talking about spells and potions that people cast and mix regardless of, and/or without connection to religious faith, we're talking about a practice, a skill, or a craft . . . so we don't capitalize it.

The spells and potions in this book are small-w witchcraft. They're intended to be easy, workable with "ingredients" that the majority of urban-dwellers have handy, and—perhaps more importantly—workable without attracting attention. You don't have to be Wiccan—or a witch—to use them.

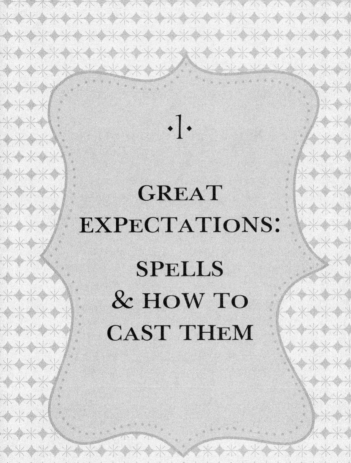

·1·

GREAT EXPECTATIONS:

SPELLS & HOW TO CAST THEM

Spells in real life aren't like the ones you might see in the movies or on TV. Without the aid of special effects, there are no flashes of fire or puffs of smoke. As much as we'd like to wave sparkles from the end of a magic wand, that's really not how magick works. Real spells work by directing energy and attention, and by following some important rules—and that's what this chapter is about.

Magickal Guidelines

Before we look at magick and spell-casting, you need to proceed with caution. When Wiccans do magick, we're guided by the Rede, "an ye harm none, do as ye will" (which is a good deal more complex than it sounds), and by the Threefold Law, which holds that what you put into the world returns to you "threefold." These guidelines—the first a moral principle, the second a law of nature—discourage Wiccans from doing magick to hurt or take advantage of others. Our magick follows these rules, and so should yours.

There *are* people who work magick who have no regard for these guidelines and believe that they are somehow exempt from the laws governing soul and society, or that these rules are impossible to follow. Some will even claim they're prepared to take the consequences of inconsiderate magick. They tend to be manipulative, untrustworthy, and unpleasant. Don't be one of them.

Here's the basic rule: do *not* do magick for or "on" other people without their specific, informed permission—even if you consider it to be helpful or loving. Do nothing to interfere with another's free will. For example: your spell to get a better job can make your resume stand out, but shouldn't intend to coerce the personnel director to hire you. Your love spell can make your best features stand out, but shouldn't compel a particular individual to find you attractive.

WHAT SPELLS ARE AND HOW THEY WORK

First, let's get the vocabulary straight. The tendency is to call every magickal working a "spell," and it's alright to use that as an umbrella concept to include a number of the different forms that magick can take. In its most extended meaning, a spell is any intentional magickal action you take to achieve a specific purpose that you may not be able to achieve by mundane methods alone. A spell is usually spoken, written, or gestured, but in practice the distinction is often blurred, and many spells involve both speaking and writing and at least one object (even if it's only the paper the spell is written on). Two other important terms to know are:

Charm: usually an item, or a collection of items often found in a pouch or other container, a charm keeps the awareness and power of a spell at your fingertips.

Potion or brew: a liquid usually, but not always, meant to be ingested. Inks or paints can also be called "brews," and special potions may be used to water gardens or houseplants, as well. For the purpose of this book, magickally enchanted bathwater can also be considered a "potion."

Now you know what spells are, but how do they *work*? The answer largely depends on whom you ask.

Some people offer elaborate explanations about energy currents—similar to the planet's wind currents—to which intentions can be attached or from which power can be drawn. Some believe spells are analogous to radio waves, broadcasting one's intent into the world, while others point out similarities to irrigation lines where a spell would draw the world's energy to your little patch of need or desire. I believe magick is a natural force, like gravity. We know that gravity actually bends space-time; perhaps magick does, too. The more thoroughly we can suspend our mature, cultural skepticism and believe that the magick will work, the stronger the image of our goal will be—and the stronger the belief, the more real the image. In turn, we begin to see the world as a place where our goal is already a reality. Therefore, gradually—very gradually, sometimes—we achieve our magickal goals.

All of these explanations presume that your goal was well defined before you cast your spell and, equally important, that your spell was ethically conceived. Again, it's at the very least wrong and often disastrous to do manipulative, vengeful, or thoughtless magick.

WHAT SPELLS LOOK LIKE

Sometimes, you know exactly what you want: a red 1968 Mustang convertible, for instance. In such cases, magick must be auxiliary to the mundane work of searching Internet sites, classic car publications, and the local paper's classified ads. Instead of "making" somebody offer their Mustang for sale, your magick could ensure that you scan the classifieds on the first day the perfect ad appears.

But sometimes, you don't know exactly what you want or need. You may express, or "define" a general goal, like mastering a golf swing or getting a new job. The magick for a new job could be a section of the want ads with your ideal job listed, folded into a copy of the cover letter you sent out with your resume, and decorated with a paper fan made out of a deposit slip, representing your first check from the new job. You could keep this charm in your bag or pocket when you go for interviews.

These magicks may work in any one—or more—of several ways. You may do a favor or good deed that reveals a hidden talent, be somewhere on an errand when a position opens up, find out that a friend knows somebody who's looking for an assistant, or get that perfect job you noticed in the classifieds and applied for. With these situations, the intent to work magick plus your visualizing having a new job, gathered energy the same way an object in space will attract objects of smaller mass to it, and eventually become a planet. The idea of a new job gradually gathers enough bits of reality to itself to actually *become* a new job.

DO SPELLS ALWAYS WORK?

The short answer is, usually, but not always the way that we expect them to. Most of the times when you think a spell hasn't worked, it's because you haven't noticed the way that it did. If you do magick for a car so you can get to and from work, and your boss offers to pay for a bus pass, does that mean your spell didn't work? Not really. The underlying need was met, so the spell did work, but in an unexpected way. Of course, your expectations have to be reasonable. If you do magick to make rain fall upwards, the chances of that working are small. If you do magick for taking a round-the-world cruise, it may take *years* for that to work.

You also have to remember that the spells you cast may not be the only "spells" at work. Your coworkers, fellow students, boss, teacher, or family members may not be doing actual magick, but they may well have an interest in the same situations you care about. They're likely to be doing whatever they can to make things turn out the way *they* want them to, which may be different than the way *you* want things to go.

People who consciously use magick have an advantage, however, over people who just want life to go their way. Magickal people understand that *everything* that happens is an opportunity. Nonmagickal people are likely to chalk something up as a "win" or a "loss," and leave it at that. But if you work magick, you know that every step is a step toward your goal, which means that in the long run, you and your magick are likely to be successful.

Kinds of Spells

There are many kinds of spells and there are many ways to cast any sort of spell, too. Some people like to have a few spells on hand—ones they can use every time a particular kind of need crops up—memorized or written down in a handy notebook, called a Book of Shadows. Others like to create new spells every time they need to do magick. Both approaches can work very well, and it's up to you to decide which one will work best for you.

In this book, you'll find general spells that you can use with just a little modification for specific circumstances, examples of different spells to use for the same kinds of needs, some suggestions for ways to personalize spells, and some guidelines for creating your own spells with materials you have on hand. However, before we look at individual spells, the places you may like to cast them, and the "ingredients" you can use, let's look at the *kinds* of spells you may want to cast.

LOVE SPELLS

Love spells can work in a number of ways. They can make you aware of situations in which Ms. or Mr. Right can notice you, and/or give you the courage to come out of your shell to get to know people who may turn out to be Ms. or Mr. Right. They can also emphasize your best qualities—the ones that will attract Ms. or Mr. Right in the first place. However, it's very important for you to realize that the ethics of spell-casting forbid you to work magick to attract specific individuals. Even if you have a crush on Johnny from Accounting or Angela from the club, you mustn't cast a spell on them. After all, you don't want them dating you because they are unnaturally compelled; you want someone whose affection for you is genuine. Instead, you can cast a spell on yourself that will work even if you don't have a specific object of affection in mind and just want to meet the right person.

PROSPERITY SPELLS

"There's no such thing as a free lunch," people say, which means that you're probably not going to get something for nothing—and greed isn't a legitimate magickal motive. It's utterly unethical to work magick for your own prosperity at someone else's expense. For example, don't use magick with the aim of getting someone fired so you can have his or her job. There is, however, more than one legitimate way of paying for lunch, so to speak, and if you have a real need and an unselfish desire, prosperity magick can help you satisfy it.

Prosperity magick is only sometimes worked for money, because our sense of "prosperity" isn't based exclusively on financial wealth. When you do prosperity magick with a particular need in mind—a job or a way to afford dinner for a special date—your magick will sometimes meet the need indirectly. An important part of prosperity magick is your willingness to stay alert to all possibilities, not just the ones you fantasize about. For example, maybe you hear about an internship or volunteer work that will lead to a paying job; or someone gives you a restaurant gift-card for your birthday, and just like that, there's dinner with that special someone.

Let's talk a little more about doing prosperity magick for yourself. Lots of people grow up hearing that while it's fine to do for others, to work for your own benefit is somehow selfish, or unworthy. Nonsense! It's absolutely true that altruism is good for us—socially, psychologically, morally, and, even physically! It's also true that you can't go very far toward meeting other people's needs until your own are met. Remember the emergency speech that flight attendants give reminding you to put your own oxygen mask on before you help anyone else with theirs? As long as you're not intentionally working for someone else's failure, it's just fine to work for your own success. Just remember that most success stories have a few twists, and be prepared for your magick to work in mysterious ways.

HEALTH SPELLS

Most healing spells are accompanied by visualizations where you imagine the patient recovering: waking from anesthesia, sitting up in bed, getting the cast taken off, walking, looking and feeling good, and so forth. Sometimes a healing visualization can involve imagining healthy cells battling the sick cells, like ninjas or knights. Almost always, there's also some tangible "medical" aspect to health magick, whether it's going to bed early, seeing a doctor, taking the correct prescription medicine, balancing the diet, or giving up smoking. Magick helps those who help themselves and the more mundane work you do towards any goal, the more energy you raise to power your magick.

Another ethical caveat here: It's always fine to do healing magick for yourself, but it's wrong to do health magick for other people without their explicit permission. It is okay, however, to send energy of love and friendship. When friends or relatives are ill, especially when gravely ill, it's tempting to cast a healing spell. But unless you've discussed it with them and they've asked you to help in that way, resist the temptation. Some illnesses cannot be cured, and to interfere magickally can do more harm than good. When you do have permission to work magick for someone else, working for "the best possible outcome" is always safe. This avoids interference with their free will, and allows healing to occur in the most appropriate way.

RELATIONSHIP SPELLS

Many people employ charms and personal ritual to ensure particular outcomes in situations involving others.

People wear "power suits" to meetings so they can negotiate with more credibility. People take deep breaths before important meetings, or make a point of eating something special before a test or evaluation, and so forth. You probably do some things like this yourself.

We call this "office dynamics" or "personality technique," and there are books written about ways to influence other people in such ways. However, some of those books don't emphasize ethics; there's a sense of "all's fair in business and war" about them. But not many people consciously understand that changing their own behavior can actually count as a *spell*. When you understand this, your range of spell-casting is vastly expanded, and your success will only be enhanced when you make sure not to deliberately hurt or take advantage of others. Remember, win-win situations never inspire revenge!

In these spells as with all others, be careful not to coerce anyone's free will. If you need to improve relations with a coworker, boss, teacher, fellow student, or family member, do so by magickally empowering *yourself* to change how you treat or respond to that person.

ORGANIZATION SPELLS

If you're anything like me, you sometimes wish you could wiggle your nose like Samantha Stevens in *Bewitched*, and have your desk, room, work, or life suddenly well organized, your deadlines met, and your phone charged and easy to find whenever you want it. You can do magick to this effect, but—like most magick—it involves some mundane work as well. The magick just makes the work feel easier and go more quickly. Surprisingly, that's often just what you need.

Many times magick depends on repetition. Even quick, on-the-spot spells tend to rely on rhyme, which is the repetition of a sound; and more elaborate rituals are traditionally repeated exactly, word for word and gesture for gesture, every time. We can learn something from this even without doing any of those rituals: routines are helpful.

HELP! SPELLS

There come times in everyone's life when you're in a jam and need some help getting out of it gracefully, with a minimum of unpleasant consequences. Of course, if you've screwed up, you have to admit it and be willing to do whatever you can to fix what you did wrong. But there are other times when the trouble you're in isn't your fault, and you need a little extra help to find your balance and get yourself back on track. Even when you're trying to fix your own mistakes, you have to pay special attention to not blaming other people. Sometimes, even if others were involved, it's best to take full responsibility.

When you're casting a spell in self-defense—if the danger to you or a loved one is clear and present and someone else is interfering with your free will, against all rules—then you may have no choice but to take whatever opportunities are available. For example, in the case of rape or armed attack, you need to do whatever works to get you through the event safely and with as little injury as possible, no matter what this means for the attacker. Of course, we all hope that the Help! spells you need are for much less dire circumstances, which they usually are.

The Basic Rules of Spell-Casting

Your spells will work, if you follow a few basic rules. The first is to use your magick ethically. There is just no getting around this one; your subconscious will know and will get in your way if you try. The other rules are:

* Know what you want, and why. Be clear, but don't clutter your imaginings with details.
* Take as many mundane steps as you can to achieve your goal. And once you've done your magick, don't spend a lot of time fretting about whether it'll work or not.
* Be attentive to signs that you're closer to your goal, and take advantage of the opportunities that come up, without taking unfair advantage of others.

There's something else you should know, and that is that any magick works better if you're prepared. That means thinking ahead. Whatever you're doing, think about what you're likely to need and make sure you have got it handy. Remember your list when you're grocery shopping, remember your claim ticket when you go to the cleaners, and so forth. If you need a spell to help get yourself together with regard to such things, keep reading! Also, remember that the bigger your magickal goal, the longer it's likely to take for your magick to work.

Your magick—like your life—will require some planning and patience. But if you're sincere about your goals (both magickal and mundane) and if they're ethical and not completely outrageous, you'll reach them—and the spells in this book will help you get there.

·2·

SPELLS
FOR THE
HEART

Love spells are, in some ways, the easiest ones to cast, but in others the most difficult. They're easy because their goal is often quite clear, and even if you don't have a particular person in mind, you still know the characteristics you want in the person you're looking for. They're difficult because you have to be careful not to manipulate anyone else. Not only is it just plain wrong to force other people, but doing so in the beginning locks you into doing it forever, which takes a lot of energy.

Love spells are also difficult because there are so many different circumstances under which love can bloom that no one spell is going to work in every situation—or even for every couple. They also often require thinking on your feet, taking advantage of opportunities that you can't possibly predict, and working with spur-of-the-moment ideas. Therefore, the spells in this section can be used as examples as well as spells that you can copy out and use over and over again. You can use them as they're written, but should also understand why they work, so you can modify them appropriately for your own life.

Before we begin, let's be clear that there's a difference between love and lust. There's nothing wrong with either one, but you need to know what you're experiencing, and what the other person is feeling, too. There are spells here that will help you find your true love—someone you can spend the rest of your life with—and there are also spells that will help you take advantage of opportunities for a good time, whether that time is for a few hours or a few months. However, whether you're looking for love or satisfying a lust, you still need to be respectful of your partner.

The fact is that, apart from any moral code, how you treat other people in love, lust, or any other relationship *is* one of the building blocks of the life that you make for yourself. If you're insensitive, thoughtless, or worse, that energy will become the hallmark of every aspect of your life. And no matter how you try to justify treating other people poorly, you won't be happy with the way that turns out for you.

In short: whether you're looking for a lifetime commitment or a short fling, don't let your prejudices get in the way. Think outside the box, and keep your mind—and heart—open when you meet people. Remember, if you can't let go of your mental control at least a little bit, no spell of any sort is going to help you satisfy your lust or bring your search for love to a happy ending.

Here are a few ideas—not spells, but the foundations for more specific magick—that you can use or modify to work in a wide variety of circumstances.

* Before going out on any date, imagine a successful conclusion—whether that's wedding bells or a couple of hours of passion. That's not being manipulative; rather it's being clear in your own mind about what you want. Remember that your own goals and the people you're involved with deserve your honesty as well, so, if you know what you want, acknowledge it when the time is right.
* If you'll be coming back to your place, put fresh flowers in the main room. Set your coffeemaker, if you have one, to be brewing at about the time you expect to be home. If it's appropriate for the occasion, set the table for two.

* If using it is part of the plan, change the sheets on your bed, and make it up the way they do in hotels: one side of the sheet folded down, chocolates (or other goodies) on the pillows. If you're so inclined, put a spray of your favorite scent under each pillow. Be safe. Have a condom handy.

In short, when you bring someone home, make your place look welcoming, as though your potential partner belongs there. As you make your preparations, sing yourself a song detailing the outcome you're hoping for. This puts the Right Vibes in the air. Remember that if you sing a bawdy little ditty, you're likely to end up with a bawdy little relationship, so if you're looking for something more, sing something more romantic.

If your date doesn't come home with you, well, then, the place is lovely for *you* and you'll be reminded that a) you are a desirable, caring, thoughtful person, and b) either you're better off on your own, or, if circumstances separated you, you'll be ready again next time. Either way, you won't have to do any work when you get home, so you'll be more relaxed while you're out. This will make you attractive and confident: you're in control of your side of things, and ready for anything.

Spells and Chants to Turn Heads

Let's look at a couple of common situations, because you're likely to find yourself in one of them.

Scenario A: You're on a date. It's wretched. You want out, but don't want to hurt your date's feelings because you wouldn't want to be dumped cruelly yourself, and apparently this person can't help being a jerk.

If it's a blind date, maybe you had the foresight to arrange for a friend to call you an hour or so into it, and give you an excuse to get up and go. If not, you can always duck into the bathroom, call a friend, and ask for a call back in five minutes. That will give you the same opportunity to say you have to leave. On the other hand, most people know about that ploy, so you probably won't be fooling your date. This offers both of you a way to save face, but it's not really magick.

In fact, this is one of those situations where the mundane solution is probably the best one to use. There's no need to cast a spell when you want out of a bad date. If you're bold enough, you can always just level with him or her, "I'm sorry. This just isn't working out, and I think it's best that we part company now."

Scenario B: You're on a date. It's going really, really well—at least, you think it is—and you'd like it to end on a positive note. Whether that positive note is agreeing to meet again or your date going back to your place, you may want to use a little magick to ensure that you wake up smiling.

Again, it's wrong to cast spells on other people, but it's perfectly alright to make yourself as compellingly attractive as possible—just like it's okay to wear your nicest clothes, or let your dinner guests smell something wonderful in the kitchen to whet their appetites.

This sort of magick falls into the category of glamoury, and can be an aspect to any type of spell. Most of us are already familiar with it in a few small ways: we use moisturizer, hair products, makeup, scent, and clothing styles to present ourselves to each other in the ways we want to be seen. (See Appendices A and B for some flavor—or scent—and color associations you might be able to use when you're deciding what to wear.) It's not falsification: we each spiff ourselves up in ways that are consistent with the aspect of our personality that we want to emphasize. This is only wrong when our intent is to defraud someone else.

You remember the story of Cinderella, right? Her Fairy Godmother dressed her up, and provided her with a coach and footmen, so that her true inner beauty would be visible to the Prince—who was, let's be honest, too blinded by his own social prejudices to notice this charming woman otherwise. But you don't need a Fairy Godmother. You can apply a spell of glamoury to yourself!

GLAMOUR BOOST

This spell takes a bit of time to prepare, but once it's prepped, you'll have it available anytime, anywhere. Begin, at home, by taking a deep breath—in through your nose, out through your mouth—and consciously relaxing. Try a couple of shoulder rolls and neck rolls. Take another deep breath.

Now, here's what you'll need:

* the nicest piece of paper (personal stationery, if you have it) in your house
* your nicest pen
* a tube of lipstick in your favorite color or a tube of lip balm, ready in another room
* tape

Flex your fingers so you can produce your nicest handwriting and settle where you can write comfortably. Sitting at a desk or table is better than leaning back on the couch with a magazine over your knees and is also more in line with the formality of this spell.

On the left side of the paper make a list of your best qualities—those you bring to a relationship. Do you have a sense of humor? Like animals? Have a green thumb? Do you volunteer? Cook? Anything you like about yourself, anything your friends and family like about you, and anything your employers like about you belongs on this list. These items can range from silly to serious, superficial to significant. This list should include your values as well as your delightful characteristics and talents. Keep each item short—one to three words at most.

On the right side of your paper, write down as many as ten qualities that you're looking for in a date or a mate. Why can the list of *your* wonderful qualities be so much longer than your potential partner's? Because you know yourself, and because you may need reminding of what a worthy person you are. Also, thinking about who you are and what you can contribute to a relationship will help you clarify what kind of relationship you want and what major qualities you want your partner to bring.

Okay, you've got your lists; the left side of the page is all about you, and the right side lists ten things about your potential partner. Now, get up. Walking with dignity, as though you're an aristocrat—important, influential, but not stuck up—go collect the lipstick or lip balm. Bring this to your desk or table, and sit back down.

Take up your pen and sign your name as you would a birthday card, not the way you'd sign a check, at the bottom of your page of lists. Make a small mark under your signature with the lipstick or lip balm.

Now fold the paper in half, lengthwise, so that the lists touch each other. Roll the folded paper around the tube of lipstick or lip balm, and holding this little package in both hands, say these words:

∞

That I am worthy shall be plain.

My goal of love I shall obtain.

To my partner foreordained,

I'll be his belle, and he my swain. *

As perfect mate I shall appear

To the one I can hold dear.

*If you are a man, looking for a female partner, use this line:

∞

She'll be my belle, and I her swain.

If you're looking for a same-sex relationship, substitute these words:

∞

I'll be the one who does endear.

Now, unroll the list, fold it again until it's small enough to tuck away somewhere private, but where it will not fade from your consciousness. It should be hidden, but in a part of your home where you spend a lot of time, and where you can be reminded of your own qualities and what you're looking for in a mate whenever your glance hits the spot where the list has been placed. You may want to tape it to your bed frame, to the bottom of your dining room table, or under a kitchen cabinet.

What you've done here is "charged" your lipstick or lip balm with the spell. Now, not only is the spell itself working, but whenever you use the balm or lipstick, your confidence in yourself will be boosted because all the qualities you bring to a relationship will be stirred up in you. Your sensitivity to potential partners will be boosted, and you'll be cued to be alert to those qualities in whomever you're with.

When you're on a date—or in any situation where you might meet Ms. or Mr. Right—use the lipstick or lip balm. As you run it lightly over your lips, do two things. Make eye contact with the other person and repeat the last two lines of the spell to yourself.

∽

As perfect mate I shall appear

To the one I can hold dear.

Instantly, the glamour will take hold and, not only will you become aware if this person is someone you may have a future with, but s/he will also be alerted. You're not forcing any feelings on anyone else—you're just waving to say hello with your pheromones, which have been triggered by the spell.

Of course, not everyone will be Ms. or Mr. Right. But even if the person you're locking eyes with isn't, s/he may know somebody, and the vibes of your glamour could inspire an introduction. Good luck!

AN ELEMENTAL DINNER

The four physical elements are Air, Fire, Water, and Earth. When you're on a date, it's easy to invoke them to ensure that things go well. You even have several options for invoking each one. Here are some ideas for you to adapt to the particular circumstances of your dinner date. To make these subtle activities work magickally, either recite this incantation silently to yourself, or "write" it over the tablecloth with your apparently randomly moving finger:

Earth and Water, Air and Fire,

Aid me to achieve desire!

Air

Air is associated with sound, scent, and ideas. Ways of bringing Air's powers to you include:

* "creative listening," which involves repeating what the other person has just said to you, slightly rephrased. They say, "I really enjoy going to football games," and you say back, "Football games are fun for you." Try to be a little more subtle, though.
* humming some tuneless notes, or part of a cheery song. If you let the other person hear you doing this as they come back from the rest room or coat check, they'll understand that you're having a good time and are unselfconscious about it. It doesn't matter whether you're entirely on key or not.
* sighing appreciatively.

* commenting on the lovely scent of the table flowers (if they're real), the other person's perfume or
  cologne, the bouquet of the wine, the smell of
  recent rain or fresh-mown grass, or the fruit at the
  farmer's market where you're strolling. . . .

Fire

Fire is associated with warmth, courage, and passion—not just romantic passion, but passion for causes
as well. One of the most obvious ways to bring Fire's
power to your date is by lighting candles, but this is not
always possible and, even if it is, you may want to give
it a little more emphasis. Other ways of bringing Fire's
power to yourself include:

* discussing causes about which you're passionate—
  if you're relatively certain that these won't be in
  opposition to the other person's interests. Politics
  may not be a good topic to bring up, but volunteering, cooking (more Fire there!), dancing, film,
  and other such subjects are usually safe.
* seeing courage in what the other person shares
  with you. It can take courage to confront a boss or
  coworker, decline a pressured invitation, try new
  foods, explore new cultural events, and so forth.
  This "courage of character" deserves recognition,
  and is something to appreciate even if the other
  person doesn't turn out to be The One.
* accepting a compliment graciously without adding
  any diminishing remarks. Never say something
  like, "Oh, it was nothing" or "I can't really take
  credit for that." Stick with "Thank you!" and smile.

Water

Water is associated with feelings, the psyche, nurture, and nourishment. For magickal purposes, any liquid represents Water: wine, juice, beer, ale, water (still or sparkling), etc. To nourish your budding relationship with this element, you can:

∗ propose a toast!
∗ gradually move your water glass across the table, closer and closer to the other person's—without impeding the dining process.
∗ get lost for a moment, gazing into the reflection of the room's lights or the table's candles in the wine or water on the table. When your attention returns to the present, explain that you were contemplating the magickal nature of good companionship.
∗ trace a drop of water down the side of a glass with your finger. This can be very sexy . . .
∗ . . . as can licking the last drop of a sip of wine or water from your lips. Such gestures must be subtle and work best with eye contact.

Earth

The element of Earth is all about strength, reliability, and practicality. Bringing Earth's powers into the mix is pretty easy. Ways to do this include:

∗ serving the other person from a bowl or plate at family dinners.
∗ opening doors for the other person.
∗ bringing a host/ess gift to an occasion at someone's home or to a party that someone is hosting at a

restaurant. This is old-fashioned—and charming in an intriguing way—and a well-chosen gift can linger in a person's memory long after the gift itself is used.

* wearing something you know the other person will like. If it's not one of your favorite items of clothing now, it may be when the relationship blossoms.

* accepting disappointment graciously. If a date is interrupted stay calm and offer reassurances that you can try it again another time, and/or find an alternative now.

* being on time or a minute or two early.

Here are a few more formal magicks—spells that are very, very easy to use toward achieving your romantic goals.

LOVE LIPSTICK

You already have some enchanted lipstick or lip balm; here's a spell to use with the mundane stuff:

∞

I say to the world that I am ready

To meet someone whose love is steady!

This [color] [balm] on my lips lets everyone read

The thought that I am available, indeed!

PRODUCT POWER

Here's something to chant or whisper while you're using gel, mousse, or other hair products:

∞

Smooth or curly, subtle or bright,

With my hair like this I look just right

For somebody who's right for me!

By my style, so shall it be!

BEGUILING GROOMING

This one's to use while you're plucking or waxing or shaving:

∞

Away goes this unwanted hair,

So there's room for what I want to be there.

Smooth my skin, clean and bright.

I'm ready if I meet [Lady] [Mister] Right!

SOCK IT TO ME

While you're putting on socks or stockings, repeat this spell:

∞

One foot, two foot, stepping out,

Love walks into my life, that's what it's about.

Adjust the heel, adjust the toe,

And soon my true love I will know.

ALLURING LOCKS

When you see someone interesting, make an adjustment to your hair—it can be a classic toss of hair over your shoulder, or the equally classic smoothing the sides with your hand. This spell is activated by movement or touch, but doing something goofy, like the stereotypically flirtatious winding a lock of hair around your finger, may well counteract the intended effect. When you toss your hair or smooth it, say this to yourself:

∞

Look at me. If you like what you see,

Meet my eye. Match my sigh.

Follow me or ask my name.

Show me, if you feel the same.

Note that this spell—while it does try to "make" the other person look at you—doesn't demand any further response. Influencing a movement that people are likely to make anyway isn't manipulative because it doesn't force anyone to do something against their interest.

TURN ON SPELL

When you're on a bus or even just walking down the street, give yourself a moment to do a 360-degree turn. If possible, change something about the way you were standing when you come back to your starting position. This may mean holding the rail with a different hand, or shifting something you're carrying from one hand to the other. As you turn and rearrange, say this to yourself:

∞

I'm turning my body and turning your head

Our views to change, our horizons to spread.

You may not be here in front of me,

But you are someone I'll soon see!

This spell shouldn't be aimed at anyone in particular, but you should pay close attention to the people you meet after you do any love spell. Even if they don't seem like Ms. or Mr. Right, there's still a chance they could be the answer to your prayers! Another version of this "turn" spell works well at parties, and goes like this:

∞

I'm turning my life and turning my head.

My view will change, my horizons spread.

Yet to arrive or in front of me,

I'll soon meet someone I should see.

If you pay attention to the small changes between these two versions, you'll get some ideas about how to modify other spells to fit the circumstances you're in.

Charms to Attract "The One"

Again, love spells are tricky. You want to be exact enough to meet your real needs, but don't want to be so particular that you overlook someone worthy. You especially don't want to charm specific individuals, because that would interfere with their free will. Instead, the best way to attract your Ms. or Mr. Right is to be seen at your most attractive. Let people see who you really are—and trust that you are your best self. Remember, love is all about who we are on the inside, not about our exteriors.

However, it's usually what people see or hear about you first that fixes their opinion. So the mundane way to charm your Prince or Princess Charming is to let him or her see you at your best—or truest—right from the start. Take a few minutes to consider what your real, passionate interests are. Do you love animals? Reading? Cooking? Skydiving? Whatever your interests, think about joining one or two clubs dedicated to those activities or volunteering for a cause—another excellent way to meet people who share your interests. It also "does good" in the world, which is never a bad thing. Remember, what we do leads to indirect consequences. Someone you meet at a volunteer session or club meeting may mention you to someone else, who remembers hearing about you during a conversation with someone else, who runs into you a year later at a business lunch, and feels both an obvious and subconscious connection. S/he may not be aware of where s/he's heard of you before, or even remember that you're the same person s/he remembers a story about, but his or her interest will still be piqued.

MEETING SPELL

For the charm itself, keep a scrap of paper with the meeting address or group logo on it handy where you can touch it. Read or recite this spell before you head out to that meeting or one of that group's-activities:

∞

Going to this [meeting] [class] [session]

Might help me find The One,

But even if it doesn't

Something worthwhile will be done!

I will meet people who all care

For things that I love too

And if that love gets personal,

And if that love is true,

Then everyone will win:

Without harm, so may it spin!

The work of being attractive to others is to be someone who enjoys engaging the world, is unafraid to give and receive, and respects social expectations without being so devoted to "fashion" that individual personality disappears. That's hard work, but that work can be helped along by magick. You already understand that it's wrong to work any magick on other people without their express permission, but that doesn't mean you can't create and carry out charms to ensure that you don't fall off anyone's radar—and that no one falls off yours.

PICTURE THIS

This is one of the easiest charms to make, but it can also be one of the most fun. You can create this charm with photos you already have on your computer, or with new pictures taken at a mall photo booth. Make sure the photos are good. Your hair, clothes, or pose don't need to be perfect, but you shouldn't look unhappy. Once you have a strip of three or four such photos, write "Here I am, my lady," or "Here I am, big boy" across the back.

Fold this photo, and tuck it into your wallet or pocket. Whenever you see or meet someone who could be your Ms. or Mr. Right, reach into your pocket and touch the photos. If they're in your wallet or bag, just touch the bag or wallet and imagine the photos within. Make eye contact with the individual who interests you, and be alert for a chance to start a conversation.

THE CHARMED COMB

Most people carry a brush or comb in their bag or pocket, and even those who don't will occasionally run their fingers through their hair in a nearly universal gesture of making sure they look "okay." Why not take advantage of this, and turn it into a magickal gesture? Enchant your comb (or brush), and it becomes a charm you can keep and use without anyone suspecting a thing!

The comb (or brush) doesn't have to be new, but it must be clean. Take time to get any stray hairs or dandruff flakes off before you put this spell on it. Turn your comb into a charm on the new (dark) Moon or on the full Moon, and repeat the process every month.

∽

In my hair leave vibes of love

And bring to me the attention of

The [man] [woman] I'm looking at

When I comb my hair and give it a pat.

Again, drawing someone's attention isn't unethically manipulative, because they're free to turn away again if they want to.

MAGICK CHARM

For this spell, you need the following:

* a button, bobby pin, bead, or penny
* nail polish (clear or red) or paint (preferably red, but any color will do)
* thread or slender string, yarn, or wire
* a small piece of paper
* pen or pencil
* small bowl or plate of water
* match
* metal container in which you can burn the paper and catch the ashes

Bring everything to a table or other work surface. On the paper, write this spell:

I am ready to find love

And I make this charm to give fate a shove.

With harm to none, and joy to all,

With this charm my love I call.

Write this spell down three times, and use slightly different handwriting each time. For example, you may first write it in your best cursive hand, then you might print it the way you would a grocery list, and the third time you may write it with your nondominant hand. (Yes, this will look dreadful, but it can represent an understanding that both mirth and trust are important qualities to bring to a lasting relationship.) Say the spell aloud each time you write it.

Now light a match and set fire to the paper, holding it over the metal container and making sure not to burn yourself. When the ashes are cool enough to touch, crumble them with your fingers.

Now, dip your penny, button, bead, or bobby pin in the water, and touch it to the ashes. Cover as much of the object as you can with the ashes, leaving only a tiny point to hold it by. When the ashes stick to the object, very carefully cover it with nail polish or paint. When the paint or polish is dry, it will have sealed the ashes of your spell onto the object. You will probably be able to see the ashes through the polish or paint; you'll at least notice the texture they create. All that's left to do is put the charm in your wallet, so it's with you wherever you're likely to meet Ms. or Mr. Right. Creating this charm on the new (dark) Moon will bring additional power to your magick. But making this charm when the Moon is waning will ensure that it will take longer to work. If you haven't met someone who interests you by the first full Moon after the charm's creation, reinforce the magick by remaking the same charm on the next full Moon. If you're doing the appropriate work, the magick should bring someone to your attention soon.

WE ARE WHAT WE EAT

Most of us have at least a few opportunities to take a plate of cookies to an event and if you think you could meet Ms. or Mr. Right at a club social, neighborhood potluck, or volunteer picnic, you can charm the cookies as you make them to encourage your true love to reveal him or herself. Making this charm involves casting two spells. Here's what you'll need:

* prepared cookie dough, or the ingredients for your favorite cookie recipe
* cinnamon
* white chocolate chips
* a heart-shaped cookie cutter or a knife

Begin by charming the white chocolate chips:

∞

Little chips, so light and bright,

And shaped like tiny kisses,

When tasted by my [Lady] [Mister] Right

Let her/him know that this is

Her/His chance to meet her/his partner true:

Chips, work as I command you to!

Follow the recipe directions (including those about preheating the oven and greasing the cookie pan)—adding the step of mixing the chips into the dough—and as you lay the cookies out on the baking sheet, cut them into heart shapes. Save the dough scraps to make one small tubular cookie. I'll tell you what that's for as soon as we finish the main batch of charm-cookies!

Just before you put the cookies in to bake, sprinkle each one with cinnamon. Do your best to make your initials with it, but don't worry if they're not actually legible. This is magick, and it's the intent that counts.

On the little tubular cookie, sprinkle the cinnamon in the shape of a heart.

When the cookies are baked and cooled, pack the heart-shaped ones to take to your event. Before you leave, eat the cookie you rolled from the scraps, saying:

∞

In finding love I'm on a roll

And I will eat this cookie whole

To say that my whole heart is in it

And my true love's heart, I'll win it.

(Remember that the color of the plate can enhance the magick, too; see Appendix B.)

Brews for Bonding

Let's be clear. When I talk about "brews for bonding," I'm not talking about slipping anybody a mickey! Putting things in people's food or drink that they don't know about is wrong, and could have legal, moral, and practical repercussions. Remember, too, that people have food allergies, and even if you want to surprise them with a new dish that you're trying out, you should ask about that ahead of time. You don't want to trigger an allergic reaction, and there's no point in literally leaving a bad taste in anyone's mouth!

With that said, let's talk about what *can* work to bond people together. Sometimes, clichés work. For instance, after a day spent outdoors in chilly weather, a mug of hot cocoa with miniature marshmallows floating on top, sipped in front of a crackling fire, is all the "brew" you need for bonding. There are times, too, when one glass or cup of soda can be a wonderful thing to share with two straws. It's a little retro, sure, but that can be romantic, especially at a diner-style restaurant.

CHOCOLATE CHARM

If you want to put a little extra magick in an already "charming" cup of hot chocolate, I recommend you do so openly, as a romantic gesture. For instance:

∞

Good hot chocolate, little 'mallows

Set the end of our day aglow.

May the warmth between us grow,

And good spirits, but not the drink, overflow.

SOUP SPELL

Everybody knows warm chicken soup is good for the body: brothy, and with enough protein to keep you going when you don't feel well. Making a cup or bowl of soup for someone when they don't feel good is a great way to bond with them. Caretaking, and being taken care of, bonds people in special ways, letting everyone know that friendship and love aren't just for "fair weather." If you'd like to add a little magick—maybe as you crumble crackers into it—here's a spell you can use:

∞

I bring you, dear, this [cup] [bowl] of soup

To ease what's thrown you for a loop,

So body and spirit no longer droop

And good health you may recoup.

This shares your helpful intention and, because you're doing your magick openly, it's neither deceitful nor manipulative. If you are by chance bringing this "brew" to someone who isn't going to recover—at least not quickly—from their illness, substitute these lines for the last two above:

∞

So your spirit, for this moment, does not droop

And my love surrounds you like a hoop.

Peculiar Potions

Don't worry, I'm not introducing eye of newt here. But there are several recipes for seldom-served warm and cold drinks to share, with ingredients that will stir emotions and enthusiasm. Tropical fruit drinks are prime candidates in this category. They're "exotic," which gives both of you a sense of having shared something special together, and energizing, which allows you to associate feeling good with the other person. There are also drinks that you can enjoy on your own, even when the person you want to bond with is not present.

With a little planning, drinks can be shared at a distance. For example, if you have to be away from home at the cocktail hour, you and your significant other may agree to pour your drinks at the same time, and toast each other before drinking. Knowing that the other person is doing the same thing can bring the two of you closer together—even if you're physically separated. Giving that sort of attention to a relationship strengthens it.

PASSION POTION, NEAR OR FAR

For this drink, each party needs:

* a highball glass
* ginger ale
* an ounce of pomegranate juice
* optional: an ounce of orange-flavored tequila
* optional: ice cubes

If you like your drinks on the rocks, start with two or three ice cubes. Then add an ounce of pomegranate juice—the juice of Persephone, the Greek goddess of Spring—into each person's glass. Our brew uses pomegranate juice to symbolize literally earth-shaking, life-changing love. If you want the potion to be "hard," add the ounce of orange-flavored tequila next. Orange blossoms symbolize love and marriage, which is why this potion includes that flavor.

Now fill the glass with ginger ale. Ginger is somewhat spicy, and the carbonation adds a bit of tingle—and both qualities contribute to a successful relationship and lasting love. Even with the alcohol, this is a relatively mild drink that won't leave you too intoxicated to share your love, in word or deed, no matter how close you are to one another.

THE MAGICK BATH OF LOVE

You've met someone. As far as you're concerned, s/he's Ms. or Mr. Right and you want to communicate on a subconscious level that you're ready to return any affection s/he feels. Even if you're in the goofy stage of love, where you worry about looking like an idiot, this spell will help you get the message across—and will give you more confidence, too.

To cast this spell, you need an evening to yourself, and a clean bathroom. It's nicer if you have a tub, but you can modify it to work in a shower, too. You'll also need:

* a candle (scented if you like)
* a nice robe or other lounge-wear
* bubble bath or bath oil
* special soap (scented, or just new)
* rose petals (optional)

Once the bathroom is as clean as it can be, bring in a candle. Next, make sure that you have a nice robe or lounge clothes ready to wear after your bath or shower. Whatever you have that feels luxurious or special to you is what you should bring out as an accessory to this magick. These clothes don't have to be conventional, they just can't be frumpy.

If you have a tub, plan on treating yourself to a bubble bath, and if you can, bring in a few rose petals. Let them float on the surface of the bathwater or the bubbles; if you're showering, set a few blooms in a vase on the floor, or on the soap dish or the rack that holds your shampoos and other accessories. Roses say romance, and the goal of this magick is to see yourself as someone both capable and worthy of a romantic relationship.

When everything is ready—the lights are low, the candle's lit, flowers are at hand, the water's running, your night clothes are ready, and the clothes you were wearing all day are in the hamper—dance your way across the room to the tub or shower. If you have a mirror in the room, look at yourself and see your body as beautiful. Reject any critical thoughts that intrude. Step into the bath or shower and luxuriate in the warm water and the scents that surround you.

As you bathe, speak to yourself in the voice of your belovéd, whether you know him or her yet or not. Admire, out loud and sincerely, the tone of your skin, the shape of your limbs. Caress yourself lovingly (not toward an orgasm—but don't feel like you've done anything wrong if you have one!), mindful that your body houses a precious being whose worth to the world is immeasurable.

When you're finished, come out of the water regally, and dry yourself with something close to reverence. Keep your thoughts focused on your best qualities, and choose to see your body as a reflection of your inner beauty. Use moisturizer before you get dressed in the special outfit you've chosen. Don't blow the candle out until you're ready to leave the bathroom—but don't forget it, either.

Thank yourself for a lovely time, and realize that you're "second-date worthy." Carry on for the rest of the evening as you normally would, but let your mind drift back to what a great time you had, the discoveries you made about how wonderful you are, and how much you have to offer to That Special Someone.

The ideal time to cast this spell on yourself? The night before, or the evening of, a date with someone you think has possibilities. If you have other things to do between the time you take this bath and the time you go on that date, you'll probably do them all the more successfully for having this reminder of what a well-rounded person you are, which will boost your confidence even more. Of course, you can modify and renew this magick as often as you like. And who knows? Maybe one day soon you'll be able to cast this spell with a working partner!

BUBBLING OVER

If you're taking just a quick bubble bath, in regular light with no rose petals, it can still be magick. Try this spell:

∞

Bubble, bubble, but no trouble —

Bath be soothing, love be double.

Clean and fragrant, warm and snug,

It feels just like a loving hug.

I'll touch toes together beneath the foam

And soon meet someone to bring home!

If we're lucky, Nature's magick or our own helps us find Ms. or Mr. Right—and also a job we can "love." But just as our partners may have a few quirks, we often find that there are one or two things we'd like to change at work, too. In the next chapter, we'll see how we can "work" some magick on the job.

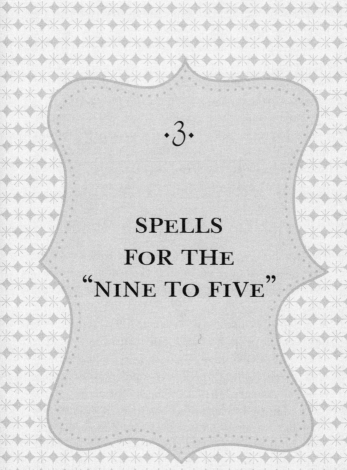

·3·

SPELLS
FOR THE
"NINE TO FIVE"

At work, control is always an issue, whether it's your own frustration or a sticky situation that needs to be taken care of. People are usually expected to be brilliantly creative in one way or another, yet disciplined at the same time. You may have to wear uniforms and work with the public, yet also be able to soothe cranky customers who're taking their bad day out on you.

Maybe you got some training when you hired on, or maybe you've learned your job on your own. Either way, this chapter will remind you that magick is one of the "tools" or "resources" you can use to maintain your sanity—and get ahead—during a tough workweek.

What Do You Have on Hand?

The first step to casting spells and making charms is to know what you have on hand. If you work in an office, you probably have a lot of common materials (pens, stapler, folders, paperclips, etc.) nearby, and much of the magickal work found in this chapter will reference these items. But if you work in a different environment, such as on an assembly line, outdoors, in a medical setting, or as a police officer, you'll have a different set of supplies and may need to make some substitutions.

If you need to substitute the items mentioned for something you have on hand, just think about the purpose the item serves. Whatever you use for the same purpose will very likely work as well. If not, feel free to make something. If you don't have a business card, for example, create a prototype using a three-by-five card, and work with that. The effort you put into making a substitute will only add power to your magick.

Money Spells

Before we look at some of the magick you can use to stay on top of things at work, let's talk about something that goes hand-in-hand: money spells. A fair number of Wiccans believe that casting money spells is wrong, and there are two reasons. First, many Wiccans believe that doing money spells is an ugly manifestation of ego. Second, many worry that bringing money to themselves will take it away from someone else, harming other people. If you agree, don't do the money spells included here. But keep in mind that you're still obligated to follow the first rule of magick—not to do it on or "at" other people without their permission—even when doing "money draw" magick. These spells don't force anyone to turn over the contents of their wallet, or to offer a raise they think is undeserved. Nor do these spells intend your own good fortune at anyone else's expense.

Are you *less* entitled than anyone else to be able to pay for the necessities of life, or *less* deserving of the occasional splurge? No, of course you're not! As long as you're not working magick to get Marlene or Dietrich fired so you can have their job, or for great uncle Aloysius to die so you can inherit, and as long as you don't want the money for some nefarious scheme to cause chaos or misery, give one of these a try and see what happens. If you end up with a windfall that makes you uncomfortable, you can always donate it to charity!

FOUND-MONEY BANK

Let's ease into it. This is a spell that I've been working for several years now, and which has always been successful. In a little box decorated with what you consider signs of prosperity and protection, save all the money you find. That includes the pennies, nickels, dimes, and occasional quarters that you find on sidewalks or in parking lots, and the money you forgot you stashed in a pocket. (If it's more than $10, I give myself a moment to remember putting it there, but if I can't remember, into the found-money bank it goes.)

To charm your found-money bank, say the following:

∞

Little bank, save [our] [my] cash

And symbolize a bigger stash.

You'll get all [we] [I] find, and it will amount

To whatever [we] [I] need in [our] [my] account.

Normally, I recharge my spells at every full Moon, but the only way I've ever recharged this one is to keep putting found money in it. When unexpected expenses have presented themselves, I've always been able to cover them.

1, 2, 3, PLENTY FOR ME

A counting spell is appropriate to use when it's more money that you need. For this particular spell you need nine pennies or other coins worth less than a dollar; but they should all be the same denomination. Here are the steps you should follow to cast this spell:

1. Stack the first three coins together, repeating "One, two, three, plenty for me."

2. Make a second stack of the next three coins, saying the same thing.

3. Repeating the rhyme once more, make a third stack.

4. Now, hold your left hand open and, with your right hand, pick up the first stack and put it on your left palm (reverse this if you're left-handed). Say "One!"

5. Pick up the next stack and put it on top of the first one. Say "Two!"

6. Pick up the last stack, and put it on top of the others. Say, "Three!"

7. Close your left hand over the coins, and tap the whole palm of your right hand over your left fist, saying "Plenty for me!" in time with the taps.

8. Turn in place, to your right, once, and say, "Harm to none, so it be done!"

9. Put these coins away in a safe place, and use them to repeat the spell monthly, or as needed.

How soon will you see extra income? Maybe not immediately, but you're not likely to find yourself suddenly strapped for funds with no options, either.

THE MONEY BRIDGE

Sometimes we find ourselves a little short between paydays. This spell is better for keeping that from happening next month than for fixing an immediate problem, but even so, you should use it when you notice a need. For this spell you need eleven pennies or other coins of the same denomination. Don't use anything with more value than a quarter.

Make two stacks of five pennies each. Place them close together that you can bridge them with the eleventh penny. There are three ways you can make the stacks:

1. All the coins in each stack can face the same way, heads or tails up. It doesn't matter which way you choose to stack; the symbolism here is that all the focus is in one direction.

2. The coins in each stack can alternate, heads and tails up. If you choose this arrangement, there should be three tails up in one stack, and three heads up in the second stack. This encourages the extra money that you're looking for to come through the ordinary channels of your life rather than in some special way.

3. The coins in one stack can be heads up and the coins in the other can be tails up. This arrangement works to induce smooth transitions between needs and funding. When you think about these three possibilities, one of them will seem more "correct" to you, and that's how you should arrange your stacks of coins.

When the stacks are ready, very carefully use the eleventh coin to make a bridge between them. Decide on the spot whether the eleventh coin should go heads or tails up. As you do this, say:

∞

Money out and money in,

Let new balance now begin

From penny up to Benjamin,

Money-luck this spell will spin.

By penny bridge I am enriched.

Abundance won with poverty to none.

Here's an alternate spell for the same bridge magick:

∞

Prosperity on either side,

Meet me in the middle with fortune allied.

Here's a bridge for coverage

So I will always be supplied.

CHARMING CHECKS

Finally, here's a spell you can work with a photocopy of your paycheck. You need a black pen or marker. If you must use another color, make sure it's not red!

Cut out the photocopied check, leaving a half an inch of white paper showing around the image. In the margin at the top of the check, directly over the first letter of your name on the PAY TO THE ORDER OF line, make three dollar signs: $$$. After that, spacing the sentences as you normally do, write the following words around the edge of the paycheck. Use your best handwriting, and instead of periods, use a dollar sign.

∞

This check is but the first of many $ They will more than sustain me $ My wealth will amass $ My finances will never impass $ Money will come $ More than a modicum $ Rightfully earned and all harm spurned $

If there is any space left over between the $ after the last sentence and the first three dollar signs you wrote, fill it with plus signs. Make sure to separate them so they don't look like one long line with vertical marks in it. (+ + + +, not ++++)

Fold the copy in half, and in half again. Put it in your wallet. As often as you can, tuck your real paychecks into this charmed copy on your way to the bank. Whenever you get a raise, redo the spell with a copy of the first check that reflects your higher rate of pay. When you replace one photocopy with another, burn the one you're no longer using, and make a minimum $10 donation to your favorite charity.

Other Spells for the Workplace

With money matters out of the way, let's move on to some other work-related situations in which a little magick could be helpful.

ONLY WORK IS WELCOME MAT

Fractious coworkers (or clients!) come with most jobs. Fortunately, when the people you work with can't be persuaded to change their behavior—or leave you alone—there are noncoercive magickal alternatives. A good idea is to put an only-work-is-welcome mat at the entrance(s) to your office space. This will keep people out unless they have a real work-related reason to be there, and it no more violates their free will than your front door does.

For this magick, you need some salt. If your office has a kitchen or employees' lounge, you may be able to find some there. Otherwise, grab some from a place that you go for lunch or bring a little from home. You also need several new or used staples.

How much salt and how many staples you need depends on how people enter your office space. You'll be dropping grains of salt and one or two staples across the width of any entrance in use. If you do most of your work from a car, for instance, you'll count each door and the trunk or hatchback as an "entrance," even if you don't regularly use all of them. Do this in the morning, ideally before anyone else arrives, but in any case, just before you start your own workday.

This can be done quite casually, and it won't look as though you're doing anything but standing in your doorway for a moment or checking to see if anything has fallen off your desk. If you don't work from a desk, you could be checking to make sure there are no hazards in your general area or you can act like you got up to do something and then promptly forgot what it was!

As you drop the grains of salt and the staples—just a few, mind you, not enough for anyone to notice the imaginary line you're drawing with them—say or think this spell:

∞

This mat of salt and steel as I toss it

Welcomes work but not any gossip!

Nothing distracting now can cross it.

Of course, at the end of the day or week, your salt and staples will be swept or vacuumed up. However, that's alright, because throughout the day you've been visualizing an actual welcome mat being in place: that bristly brown material that people can wipe their feet on with the charm-words written on it in bold black letters. You know that anyone who comes toward you desk will feel the energy of your intent, and will hesitate for just an instant.

If it's not something work-related that brings them to you, they may think better of it and go away before entering your space. If they barge right on through, the energy will cling to them, and they'll find themselves more and more uncomfortable. It shouldn't be too tough to encourage them to turn right around. The best way to do this is to not respond to their irrelevant conversation. You may look up and smile pleasantly, as though you've seen them passing your office or your station as they should have done. By not interacting with them, you'll provide them with the quiet they need to notice your only-work-is-welcome mat. As soon as they become aware of it, they'll take their nonwork business elsewhere.

I'M APPRECIATED

Oftentimes, supervisors bring only complaints to our work stations. It's well established that sharing only criticism with others lowers the quality of their work, but some bosses still think that berating employees will help. Anyone who works with higher-ups like this longs to hear, at least occasionally, that they do a good job and are an important part of the team. It's unethical to try to force the manager to change, but it's alright to create an atmosphere in which expressing appreciation is easy for most people.

For this magick, you need a small bottle of baby powder. There may not be any in the office supply closet, but you can find it at any drugstore. Again, you'll cast this spell privately, preferably before anyone else enters your space on a given day.

As you sprinkle the baby powder around your desk (so lightly that it's hardly visible), say

∞

Coming here makes people smile

And think, just for a little while,

Of what is good and has been done right,

And think to say so — before they bite!

For satisfaction all 'round, this spell I ground.

Because the powder will be vacuumed up later, you may like to put a little at the bottom of your pencil holder, or in a drawer, as well. Don't forget that you're casting the spell on yourself, too, so you'll feel like letting your boss and coworkers know what you appreciate about their efforts.

Quick-as-You-Like Spells

Exasperated? At the end of your rope? On the verge of doing something rash that could make matters even worse? You need something that works quickly, with less than five minutes of preparation. One of these Quick spells could be just the thing! These particular bits of magick aren't spoken-word spells as much as they are body-language spells. They work whether you're sitting or standing and their purpose is to change the focus of a conversation or situation. And of course, because it's unethical to work magick on other people without their permission, they work to change our perspective first.

Just remember that when you change the way you see things—in this case literally—your behavior changes, which means that other people's responses change, too. You're not forcing them to do anything against their will, you're just changing their environment so a different behavior will work better for them.

"Quick-as-You-Like" is a category of spell, and includes an infinite number of movements, ranging from subtle to grand. As you read on, you may begin to think "this isn't magick, this is psychology!" Just remember that the human psyche is known to communicate symbolically, and it *is* the realm where magick works! You'll need to adapt these ideas, or maybe come up with your own, to meet your own very specific needs. These body-language spells (all of which do include some verbalization) can be used individually or in combination.

EAST, THEN SOUTH, THEN WEST, THEN NORTH

You're talking to a coworker, or a customer, who is in your face about something that's neither your fault nor your responsibility. Maybe it's about something that you need to fix, but she's too upset for solutions to be considered, much less implemented. If you match her anger, you'll only escalate the situation . . . and you may draw the boss's ire, too.

For this spell to work, you need to be standing up. Take a quick step—not backwards, but sideways—and turn your body so you're facing her profile. It will only take her a second to follow your turn, but in that instant before she does, you've got a new perspective on her anger. She's likely to turn her head first, and then her body, and for that split-second, her attention will be slightly distracted from haranguing to coordinating her movement. And when you're both in your new positions, you'll be seeing something different in the background.

By casting this very physical spell in a situation where standard or mundane office protocol is ineffective, you're performing a deliberate action that doesn't have any direct connection to your goal, other than your intent to make the exchange more useful. You use natural energies—both gravity (moving) and psychology—and you change your surroundings in a way that benefits you without harming anyone else.

THE WONDER WALTZ

This spell keeps you in front of the person, but the visual cue of dancing redirects both your energy and your "partner's" and will leave both of you the opening that you need to bring the confrontation down a notch.

If you are at your desk, across a table from the other person, or otherwise seated before him, you can move your body from the waist up, forward and to the side, or back and to the side. Your "partner" is likely to either turn toward your movement, or mirror your "steps." Either way, the physical change of position will give each of you a new perspective, and the momentary distraction will give you an opportunity to "dance" away from the unpleasantness of the encounter.

THE NOD-AND-GLANCE

This spell works only if you are paying attention to the grievance being brought to your attention. If the complaint is bogus and the other person knows that, then taking it seriously puts him or her at a disadvantage; if the other person is sincere, then s/he will appreciate your respect. However, if *your* intent is to mock the other person, this spell will do you no good in the long run, and may do you considerable short-term harm.

Listening carefully to what the other person is saying, express your understanding or agreement with a nod. Do this three times. As you are nodding for the fourth time, glance at your watch, or something over the other person's left shoulder. Using the person's name, ask him or her to meet you later to finish brainstorming. Use that term, "finish brainstorming." If you're standing or in a public area when you cast this spell, move away when you're through. If you're sitting down at your desk, or a conference or cafeteria table, turn your attention to something else.

"Brainstorming" is a term with two meanings. One is medical, and refers to neurons firing out of control. The other is cultural, and refers to a method of problem-solving in which ideas are brought up—without editing—until there are several to consider, one of which is likely to work. By using this term, you can turn the out-of-control energy we're confronting to solution-oriented sharing, which is always the goal!

THE FLISH

Begin by holding the middle finger of one hand with the thumb and first two fingers of the other, as if you'd just gotten a paper cut on the cuticle of the middle finger. As you do this, think hard about your immediate need. Do you want to correct a mistake? A coworker to turn down her radio? Squeeze that thought into your finger.

Now, curl that and the other fingers on that hand toward your palm, so that the nail of your middle finger rests on the end of your thumb, and then flick your fingers back out again, so fast that it makes a sort of "flish" noise against the skin of your thumb. If you want to say or think magick words as you do this, try "flishplanation," for a chance to explain or "radio flish," for the noise reduction. This unobtrusive spell works by gathering the energy of your desire into your curled fingers, and then releasing it outward towards its physical goal with your "flish" movement. Remember to aim the energy at an object, not at a person.

THE MAGICK FINGER WIGGLE

The Magick Finger Wiggle is a gesture that's become such a part of the culture that you may even be able to do it in full view of your coworkers, although it shouldn't be aimed at any of them. To cast this spell, extend both hands, palm down. Aim your fingers toward any inanimate object that's causing trouble, whether it's that coworker's radio, a recalcitrant copier, or even a stuck elevator! Glare at the object, and wiggle your fingers for just a couple of seconds. The offending object will probably behave more acceptably afterwards: something less obnoxious will come on the radio, or someone else will ask that it be turned down; the copier will at least tell you what's wrong with it if it doesn't start working again; or the elevator will arrive within a few seconds.

THE SAMANTHA STEVENS SPECIAL

Contrary to popular belief, Samantha Stevens, the heroine of *Bewitched*, didn't wiggle her nose. She twitched her lips, and anybody can do that. It's another iconic gesture in our culture, which means you can get away with it in public, especially when the goal of your magick is likely to be obvious. Has the toilet in the washroom backed up? Is someone in your parking space? Twitch your lips. Your results won't be instantaneous, but before long, the situation will change.

Even Quicker Spells

These *are* spoken-word spells. They're easy to learn, easy to modify, and you can say them, think them, or sing them to whatever tune you like. Even reading these spells can activate them and once you read them, you'll probably come up with ideas for more.

COPIER INCANTATION

∽

Copier, copier, I need you, yes I do!

No more jams: don't be a lion, be a lamb.

WORD PROCESSING "WOOJIE"

∽

Be a nice program, there you go —

Don't eat my work, just let it flow!

I will back up, and I'll save,

And all about your features rave!

SUPERVISOR SPELL

Boss, oh boss, o lovely boss,

Sometimes I think you're an albatross.

But today I'll see you at your best

And be able to work with extra zest.

COOPERATION INCANTATION

Hey, nonny, nonny — time is short!

I sure could use some more support!

Safety Spells

As you recite either of these spells to yourself, imagine that you're surrounded by an invisible bubble, which acts as a personal shield and keeps a comfortable distance between you and anyone else.

Both of these spells—and any that you compose for yourself—need to be sealed. Seal every spell the same way, or each one differently. A seal that many Wiccans use is "with harm to none, my will be done," which is both an affirmation and a command. You can seal a spell physically, too, with a snap of your fingers, or three quick taps of your finger on the back of your hand or an object; something made of real wood is ideal. Have you heard the sayings "touch wood" or "knock on wood?" From a probable beginning as a spell-seal, this way of connecting with and drawing power from Nature has become a spell, for luck and/or protection, in its own right.

SAFETY SPELL I

∞

No weird people on the bus*

Will give me any trouble

For as I power my aura up

I'll have protection double.

*Change the word "bus" to your mode of transit.

SAFETY SPELL II

∞

I walk in a space that's just for me,

Within a shield no one can see.

My boundary's safe; I've room to move,

And no one comes in unless I approve.

Chants

∞

Chants can be tuneless; chants can be sung.

They can be cute, and they seldom go wrong.

They're meant to be repeated, several times

*And they don't have to be in perfect meter
or the greatest of rhymes.*

That's a chant, and you may use it to build your confidence toward composing one of your own. Chants take many forms and even when they don't have a tune, there's a sort of sing-song quality to them because of their rhythm. They're usually short, easy to remember and to vary by a word or two, are most often repetitive. Each chant should be repeated at least three times.

When do you need a chant? Whenever you're frazzled, discouraged, oppressed, gloomy, isolated, overwhelmed . . . you get the picture. Chants, which can be like mantras, help us refresh and reconnect with our vitality. Some of these chants are patterned after commonly used Wiccan chants, others are original to this book. Feel free to pick and choose among them, and to modify them for your own needs. If you want to make up your own, go for it!

'EVEN IF YOU CAN'T SING' CHANT I

My spirit dances in joy through the noise,

How light are my steps!

My heart is glad beyond the madness,

How light are my steps!

'EVEN IF YOU CAN'T SING' CHANT II

Nine to five, nine to five,

Through the day I will survive.

Five to nine, five to nine,

I shine in the hours that are mine.

'EVEN IF YOU CAN'T SING' CHANT III
∞

Night shift, my shift, and I shift my shape,

It's a gift that I can shift; who I am is my escape.

'EVEN IF YOU CAN'T SING' CHANT IV
∞

I am a river flowing, carving through the rock,

Tracing beauty where I go, giving all things life.

'EVEN IF YOU CAN'T SING' CHANT V
∞

This is me: I'm breathing; my heart beats,
my blood flows.

I'm sharing my life and my power, and as I do,
my mind grows.

This is me: I'm giving, I'm living, I'm glowing.

'EVEN IF YOU CAN'T SING' CHANT VI
∞

There's an opportunity brewing.

I'm doing my best today, renewing

My quest all ways.

'EVEN IF YOU CAN'T SING' CHANT VII
∞

Carpool, appointments, tedium, emergency, per diem,

Overtime — VACATION!

Charms for the Workweek

These charms are easy to make, and they keep working. Once you've created one, it will serve you for several weeks. You can then either "recharge" the one(s) you've got, or make new ones. In most offices, break rooms, or supply closets, there's a lot of material to work with. By using this "stuff" in various combinations, you can make a charm for darned near anything.

A CHARM TO KEEP THINGS UNMOVED

No matter where you work, your desk or station is at least sometimes vulnerable to disturbances by your bosses, coworkers, or a cleaning crew. Sometimes, your own ideas about "organization" may make files or accessories hard to find. This charm will help—and you can prepare it at home if you don't work in a conventional office or don't want to be seen fiddling at your desk. Begin by collecting:

* two sticky notes of equal size
* four paper clips (choose a color that represents order and/or protection to you)
* one of your business cards (you can sketch one if you don't use business cards)

On the back of the business card, write with a pen or permanent marker:

∞

This is my desk [station], and mine alone,

Disturbance and disorder begone!

Use any color you like, but don't use a pencil because you don't want anyone or anything to be able to erase this command. Naturally, you want your handwriting or printing to be as neat as possible.

Put one paper clip on each side of the card and arrange your sticky notes before you, sticky sides up and opposite each other. Put your business card in the middle of one of the notes; fold the card in half (or more) if you need to in order for it to fit. If you do need to fold it, fold your charm-words to the inside. Now put the other sticky note on top of the one your card is on, with the sticky strips on opposite sides, so the two pages stick themselves together, covering your card. As you do this, repeat the words you just wrote on the card (under your breath or in your head if need be).

If you have serious problems with disturbance and disorder on your desk, you can write those words again on both sides of the sticky "envelope" you've just made for your business card. If you do write them again, repeat the words either aloud or to yourself.

Next, seal the other two edges of your sticky-note envelope with tape. Say the charm-words once more as you do this. In the same neat writing that you used for the charm-words, write the date on both sides of this packet, and initial it. Now stand up, and holding your charm in both hands turn around in place three times, or walk around your space three times, moving clockwise, and then put the charm at the bottom of a desk drawer, the back of the calendar, or somewhere else unobtrusive *at your desk*.

If you don't have a desk, or can't stand up and move around in your work space, hold the charm in both hands, raise your hands as high over your head as you can, and make the fullest possible circle around your space with your hands. Then put it somewhere safe and close to where you work. Will that be under your chair? In the glove compartment? In your wallet? Take a moment to think about it, and you'll know the best place. If your coworkers notice any of this, you can just smile as though you're wondering what you got up to do (everybody understands that!), or turn your arm-circle into a stretch.

You'll know it's time to replace your charm if and when it comes loose from its spot or gets severely crumpled or torn wherever you've put it.

AURA OF SERENITY

In some work environments there are times when you're not in your office and still have to deal with the office crew. Some workers have no office, but feel the need for a little personal space. In those cases, the Aura of Serenity charm will give you the advantage you need. Begin by collecting:

* a facial tissue which you've moistened
* a dry facial tissue
* something to represent yourself. The simplest object is your business card, or your initials on a scrap of paper. But a lipstick print, a dab of sweat, or a dab of the lather you use to wash your hands—on a separate piece of tissue—will work just fine.
* tape or a rubber band
* Wite-Out

On the object you've chosen to represent yourself (the business card or the tissue dabbed with lipstick, sweat, or soap suds), make little dots with the Wite-out in a circle or an oval around your name on the card, your initials on a piece of paper, or the "dab" on a tissue. Allow the fluid to dry. If you don't have Wite-Out handy, you can use a pen or marker. Yellow is a good color. Think of these dots as your aura of serenity, surrounding whatever represents you as they'll surround you yourself. Holding your object, sit or stand comfortably and take three deep breaths: in through the nose, out through the mouth—a standard relaxation technique. As you take these breaths, visualize yourself being surrounded by the aura that you've "drawn" on your card, paper, or tissue. Enveloping your body, this aura may feel like the air on a pleasant spring day, or a cozy afternoon around a fire.

When you've taken your deep breaths and visualized your aura of serenity, pat your object with the moistened tissue, then pat your temples and/or the insides of your wrists with the same tissue. Doing this creates a physical connection between you, your aura of serenity, and the object that magickally represents the aura. None of these gestures need to be broad enough to attract any attention.

Finally, put your object and your moistened tissue together, folding as necessary (printed side of the business card in the center of the fold), and gather them up in the dry tissue. Close this "pouch" with a piece of tape or a rubber band. Tuck it in your purse, bag, or pocket. Before you let go of your object, repeat these words, in a whisper, under your breath, or in your mind:

∽

Coworkers, bosses, and clients can be

Frustrating to each other but not to me,

For I'm in an aura of ser-en-i-ty.

In moments when other people may count to ten, you can repeat this rhyme to remind yourself that you're protected. Being made of tissue, the physical form of this charm won't last very long. This is as it should be, for as it tatters, its power will become part of you. Eventually, nothing will be left of it; if you used a business card, even that will fade and shred. Take this wear and tear as a sign that you're absorbing the aura of serenity and making it part of your life.

POST HASTE
If you normally write letters or notes as part of your job, you'll be able to make one of these charms as often as you need to. In fact, the Post Haste spell bridges the gap between charms and other magick because, although it will function as a charm as long as you leave the envelope unopened, its magick can start working as soon as you sign the letter. You can also intend for it to work when you seal and stamp the envelope, drop it in the mail chute, or pick it up from your mailbox. You can even direct it to release additional magickal energy at each of those times!

What is this letter going to say? Since this spell is related to work, try to use company letterhead, but if you can't or it doesn't feel right to you, begin by writing the company's name and address across the top of a sheet of paper. Using the format you'd use for any company letter, date it, and address it to yourself. The letter should look like the following:

> *Letterhead*
>
> *Date*
> *Your name*
> *Your home address*
> *Dear (Your name):*
>
> *This is to let you know that, partly due to your efforts, the situation you've been concerned about at work has been resolved, satisfactorily to all parties. Everyone's needs will be met.*
>
> *Sincerely,*
> */s/*
> *The Management*

Write "**/s/**" where a signature would normally appear. This charm will begin to work as soon as you take this letter from the printer and read it; it will continue to work as you fold it and get it ready to mail.

If you want to use it as a charm, don't open it when the mail carrier delivers it to your home address, but put it in your bag or briefcase until you begin to see it manifesting at work. If you want to throw one big bolt of magick at the problem, open it when it's delivered with your mail, and hop around your house or apartment as if you'd just won the Publisher's Clearinghouse Sweepstakes.

Potions to Brew at Work

Unless your office throws a Halloween party, you're probably not going to be stirring anything up in a cauldron. But on a tense day, concentrate on lightening things up when you stir creamer into your coffee! Even if all you can have is a bottle of water at your work station, you can use the old-fashioned magick of brews and potions to make at least a few hours of your day more pleasant.

Whether or not you put anything *in* your "brew," you can infuse it magickally by stirring your intent into it. Whatever you use to stir with—a spoon, plastic stick, or straw—will conduct the energy of your visualization into the liquid. If stirring's not an option, you can use any of these as a *swirling* spell instead. That way, you can use one with an after-work drink if you need to.

Generally speaking, stirring or swirling clockwise adds power to a brew, and stirring or swirling counter-clockwise gives the brew the power to diminish. For example, if you want to build your energy or immunity, stir or swirl clockwise. If you want to reduce the power of a cold or your level of frustration, stir or swirl counter-clockwise. According to your need, try any of these— or compose one of your own.

YOU ARE WHAT YOU . . . DRINK!

∞

Into my drink goes what I think:

I think today will be good for me.

Work will be done, woes will be gone;

As I will, so mote it be.

FEEL BETTER BREW
∞

This brew is hot and healing.
This brew will bring relief.
My health no one else's is stealing,
And discomfort is made brief.

MOOD MAGICK I
∞

Stir to the right, mood be light!
Stir to the left, gloom be cleft!

MOOD MAGICK II
∞

Stirring clockwise, faster and faster
Brightens the day and avoids disaster.

ENERGY ENCHANTMENT I
∞

Stirring the brew, caffeine-free,
Stirs me too: the energy's in me!

ENERGY ENCHANTMENT II
∞

Stirring, stirring, counter'wise, *
Winding the energy up
So constructively 'twill arise
When I drink it from this cup!

*A poetic abbreviation, short for "counter-clockwise."

CONCENTRATION CONJURATION I

∞

Important interactions are at hand.

Stirring, the Waters of Life I command.

Confident rivers and powerful sea:

This drink brings their strengths to me.

CONCENTRATION CONJURATION II

∞

Many things are on my mind.

I stir to the left my cares to bind,

So I can focus on work at hand

And of myself be in command.

Note that only one of these stirring spells—the first one—has a built-in seal, "so mote it be." You'll need to add a seal to any of the others that you use.

Water Potions

Most people keep water on hand throughout their work day. No matter what kind of bottle your water is in, if it's plain or flavored, or if it's a sports drink, you can always enhance it with magick. You can also use these spells in any aspect of your life, and with any kind of container that you use at work, home, or play.

WATCHFUL WATER

You can add protection to your water by enchanting the lid of the bottle. Put the lid on its round edge in front of you on your desk. With your dominant hand, roll it away from you as far as you can, saying:

∞

Keep out all that would impair

As you roll it back towards you, finish the rhyme:

∞

Bring in good, and thirst repair.

For this spell, "thirst" means physical dryness that can be relieved by a quick sip, but it also means any other need you have—for knowledge, materials, or conditions to complete your work properly and on time.

When you twist the lid back onto the bottle, now and in the future, such as when you've taken it off to refill the container, say:

∞

Water clear, mind clear:

Nothing to choke me happening here.

In this context, "choke" means not only taking a drink down the wrong pipe, but also to anything that will stymie the work you're doing.

COUNT ON IT

If numerology appeals to you, you can use your "name number" to make your water bottle a reservoir of personal power, from which you can sip any time. All you need for this and the following spells are the charts in Appendices C and/or D, your water bottle, and a permanent marker. (Something like a Sharpie works especially well because it has a small tip that's easy to write with.)

Appendix D gives you a table of letter correspondences to numbers that you can use to find the numerical value of your name. There follows a chart of the significance of each number. If you're looking for a particular strength or quality, experiment with different spellings of your name until you find one that equals the appropriate number.

Then all you need to do is write that number somewhere on your bottle, saying:

∞

Magick number of my name,

Fill me with your power.

I drink and energy reclaim;

I count on blooming like a flower.

You may want to put your name on the bottle, too, in case coworkers need to know it's yours and not up for grabs. The pun in the word "count" adds a little extra zing to the spell, especially if you repeat that line to yourself every time you take a swig.

NOW YOU KNOW YOUR ABC'S

If numerology's not your "thing," you can work with the magickal power of your name. In Appendix C I've created a table of letter correspondences, based partly on the meanings of Runes. Look up the meaning of each letter of your name, and see what strengths they give you in combination.

Use this spell as you write your name on the bottle. (Feel free to make your letters plain or fancy.)

∽

In my name, every vowel

Will keep my work from going afoul.

And every consonant I write

Will keep my power at its height.

FLAVOR BUFFER

If you drink flavored water, refer to the chart in Appendix A for a list of qualities associated with various flavors. When you know what your chosen flavor can do for you, call up its power by swirling the bottle slightly (clockwise, of course), before you take a drink, and say this to yourself:

∽

[Quality of the flavor] in my water,

Empower me now: do not falter.

By using these spells, you won't have to experience the workplace as the horrible environment that cultural stereotypes say it is, but even so, you're probably glad to put the work day behind you and head for home. In the next chapter, you'll find some spells to make your "home sweet home" an even happier place.

·4·

SPELLS
FOR THE HOME
SWEET HOME

Although our homes share many features and routines, there are lots of ways that your home—like you—is uniquely individual. Home is where you keep everything from clothes and household goods to important papers. Home is where your pets live, and the place your children will remember when they're out on their own. Home is also where the unexpected can happen, and where we sometimes need help to keep things on track.

If you end up in a difficult situation and can't find the exact spell you need in this chapter, remember that you can modify any spell to meet your personal needs.

Spells and Chants to Keep It Together

One thing we all have in common, with no exceptions, is the clock. No one's clock gives them more than twenty-four hours in a day and virtually all of us wish, at least sometimes, that it did. If you're lucky, you have a few open days on your calendar, but there are times in everyone's life where it seems impossible to get everything done properly and on time.

If you feel out of control and need help getting your act together, try these simple spells:

SQUIDGING THE SCHEDULE

Squidge is a combination of "squeeze" and "fiddle" and "nudge," and it means to creatively adjust. That's what you're going to do here. To begin, open your daybook or calendar to the busiest pages, the ones that have you worried about falling behind. Put both hands on the pages, with your fingers spread wide to cover them. Say:

∞

So much to do, so little time!

Take a deep breath, schedule of mine.

Show me a squidge that will make it all fine.

Leave the pages open overnight. When you look again in the morning, you're likely to see that an appointment can be moved, or an errand shifted, to make things a little easier. You may even get news of a deadline being extended, or something nonessential but time-consuming being cancelled altogether!

TIDY, NOT TEDIOUS

Cleaning can seem daunting, especially after a hard day at work. But coming home or waking up to a tidy house can help you begin or end a day on a positive note, so it's worth the effort it takes. When housework has gotten away from you, even thinking about taking care of it, much less doing the work, can make you grumpy—not the result you're looking for! This spell will help, and if you'd like, you can turn it into a chant by singing it.

In one room of your home, choose three things that make the worst impression of "mess" in the room. As you pick or wipe them up, say or sing these words with whatever final line works best for you:

∞

One little, two little, three little put-aways.

One little, two little, three little clean-ups.

One little, two little, three little rearranged.

Makes a perfect [evening] [visit] [party] [finish]!

OR

∞

Then I will be mellow!

If you're cleaning because you appreciate tidiness, speak or sing about being mellow, because that's your reward for the work. If you're expecting guests on short notice, try the other line as you'll want to be sure that your work contributes to the success of the visit. You'll need to say or sing these lines two or three times, depending on how long it takes you to put things back where they belong. But with this spell, even though you don't have time or energy to clean thoroughly, the work you can do will have the same effect as if you'd spent hours.

DUST IN TIME

If you've been brought up to think that nothing less than a full day's housework will do, you've probably stressed out a number of times about all the work you haven't done. You may have figuratively cringed at the thought of dust bunnies attacking your guests, or having someone see an unmade bed or a wrinkled place mat. If that sounds like you, here's a spell to help you chill out:

Sit down. Take three deep breaths, in through your nose and out through your mouth. Picture sunlight streaming in through a window into your favorite room in your home. Remember happy laughter and sincere smiles. With those sounds and images in your mind, say:

∞

Let the dust bunnies live under the bed

And I'll live among my friends instead.

Now say the spell again, take three more deep breaths, and have a good time with your friends, no matter where you're meeting them. Be sure to notice how cheerful your home feels the next time you come home.

SHINING STAR SPELL

Magickal people know that the power for magick—and the power for successful mundane work, too—comes from our confidence that we matter in the world, beyond our roles as workers, parents, or spouses. However, we all need an occasional reminder that we're important to the universe. This recharging enchantment reawakens that awareness. Take a piece of paper—it doesn't matter how big it is—and draw a star. Decorate it any way you like, but do decorate it. When you're done, put the number twelve at the top, the number six at the bottom, and the other numbers of a clock face in their proper positions around the star. In the middle of the star, write your initials. As you write your initials, say:

Twenty-four hours is all there are

To sleep, eat, and work . . . and shine like a star!

When you cast this spell on yourself, you'll remember that you are the star of your own life, and that recognizing your own value is as important as sleeping, eating, and working.

ANGERS AWAY

When things get out of hand at home, getting angry is a common response. Most of us know that getting

angry almost never helps, and very rarely makes us feel
any better, either. Decades of scientific studies have
shown that social stress increases aggression, but if you
don't have the time or money for therapy or retreat
weekends, this spell can help.

Sit down somewhere comfortable. Beginning at
your feet and working upward, through your legs, trunk,
arms, and neck, tense your muscles and then relax
them. Take three deep breaths, in through your nose
and out through your mouth. If possible, close your
eyes. If not, look at your lap. Say:

∞

Deep breath, deep breath . . . close my eyes.

No need to let my temper rise.

I am not against the wall.

This isn't so important after all.

You're not putting a spell *on* yourself so much as
you're taking a spell *off!* Remember, nine times out of ten,
the things that annoy us are not really worth getting upset
about. That's what this spell does: it lets your magickal
self shake off the illusion that whatever's bugging you is
important enough to risk your blood pressure for.

CONTROLLING CONTROL

For some of us, home is the one place where we are
in control. At work, the boss is in charge. On the com-
mute, it's the conductor or that guy in the car up ahead
who thinks he's the only one on the road. However, at
home, it's all up to us. So when someone interrupts our

reign with a need or idea that wasn't part of our plan, it can be upsetting.

Sometimes it's an urgent need that you're happy to help take care of, or a good idea you're happy to accept. But it may seem like a deliberate challenge, or be an idea that you just don't want any part of. In those cases, you need to stay calm, but be able to opt out or even dissuade someone else. Here's a spell to cast quickly when you're in one of those situations.

To be in control I don't need to freak out.

I can stay calm without being weak.

I can speak quietly without any doubt.

When this spell's in effect, you can say, "No, you may not take the car," or "I don't want to go out for pizza, but I hope you'll come back for dessert when you're done," or even "Joe, call 9-1-1 and let them know Aunt Myrtle's broken her wrist." Anger would only invite argument or generate confusion, but under this spell, your authority will put you in control and keep everything on track.

EXER-SPELL

Plans can change in all sorts of ways. You need to be able to deal with these changes—like an extra person suddenly coming to a long-planned event, an emergency that needs your attention, or even a surprise party—because you don't want to clutter your home with "vibes" of discontent. Here's a spell that works both physically and emotionally.

Stand with your feet as far apart as your shoulders are wide. Put your left hand on your left hip, and reach your right arm over your head, toward the left, as far as you can. You'll be bending over to your left side. Now reverse your arm positions, and stretch to the right. Repeat the whole sequence, and the third time (third time's the charm!) you do this exercise, say:

Flexibility is my friend.

My plans must change, but the world won't end.

You can cast this spell with other stretching exercises if you like, but not with anything like jogging in place or lifting weights. It's flexibility you're after, and your movements must be consistent with that goal.

When you're done with the three stretches, clap your hands three times. Then move your feet out a little farther, and spread your arms wide. If you like, you can stretch your shoulders now, but the important thing is to hold that open position for a count of nine—a magickal number. (Nine is considered magickal because it's three times three, and three is a magickal number. Three is magical because there are three realms, variously identified as earth, sea, and sky; physical, psychoemotional, and spiritual; past, present, and future, etc.) This will leave you mentally and physically flexible, and "open" to the change in your plans.

UNIVERSAL SOLUTION

Some days, nothing goes right. We have too much to carry, and drop some of it. We can't find our keys, credit cards, or glasses. The elevator gets stuck, an appliance malfunctions, the paper's not delivered. . . . If one thing goes wrong, it's easy to chuckle about it. If two things go wrong, you may start making jokes about bad luck or karma. By the time three or more things go wrong in a single day, you may not think it's all that funny—and could use a spell to get the universe back on your side again. Here's just such a spell. This time, say the spell and follow it up with the gestures. Don't worry if the examples in the spell aren't exactly what's going wrong for you. They represent all kinds of goings-wrong.

If you're at home, lie down on your bed. If you're out, find a place where you can sit or stand with some privacy. Say:

∞

Spot on my shirt, hole in my sock,

Key won't fit into the lock . . .

I'll laugh, I'll dance, I'll start again,

And time and tide will be my friend.

Now, make the universal gesture of sleep: press the palms of your hands together, put them against one side of your face, and close your eyes. Then mime waking up. Stretch a little, blink, yawn, and smile. If you're on your bed, actually get up. Now laugh. If forcing a real laugh is beyond you, say "ha ha," but make sure it's sincere. Do a quick little dance—a jig, a cha cha, or even just a hop from one foot to the other. Now say, "What a beautiful day," and carry on. You'll have started over, reset the day's mood, and things should go much better from now on.

GUM CHARM

The same way many people carry a flashlight and some extra change in our cars, it's helpful to have a couple of charmed objects on hand for use at a moment's notice. You can use nearly any object that you'd like, but I suggest laying a spell on a pack of gum, and another one on something of your own choice that you can always have with you.

To set a spell on sticks of gum that you'll be chewing some time later, you may leave the package unopened, or you can open the pack or box and work with the individual pieces. Hold the packet or pieces in your right hand, and raise your left hand over your head. This allows the power for your spell to enter your body through your left (or "receptive") hand, and lets you transfer it into the gum with your right (or "projective") hand. If you're left handed, hold the gum in your left hand and raise your right hand over your head. Say:

∞

By the Earth in the sap of the tree,

By the Fire of the sun's bright glance;

By the Water that nurtures the root,

By the Air in which the leaves dance;

The gum that is made from this plant

Will ever my magick advance.

Power rise as I chew, flavor release the spell,

My need be met, no harm beget

And all distress be quelled.

When you need to, take out a stick of your enchanted gum and, as you begin to chew, say:

❦

I'm not gonna lose it, whatever comes —

'Cause I am chewing my magickal gum!

TOKEN MAGICK

To enchant an object—a token—to work as a charm whenever you need it, hold the chosen object in your "power" or "projective" hand, raise your other hand overhead, and say:

❦

By Sun and Moon and each Compass tower,

Feel the charge and hold the power.

By nine times nine and three times three,

Keep the magick safe for me.

When I conjure with this in my hand,

Release the power to my command.

Keep this object handy wherever you are, and when you need it, hold it and say:

❦

Children holler, partner's at a loss,

Every wire seems to be crossed.

I give my enchanted _____ a toss,

And then I find the perfect poss-

Ibility: hurray for me, so mote it be!

Toss your token three times, and wait three minutes. By then, a solution to your problem will at least begin to glimmer in your mind, and you'll be able to take it from there. If actually tossing it would risk losing it, just turn it over in the palm of your hand. And don't worry if the frustrations described in the spell aren't exactly the ones you're experiencing. They're symbolic.

Charms for a Delightful Dwelling

Even for people who aren't neat freaks, clutter is stressful—and entertaining can be even more so. Don't worry! You can cast a spell to make every party a success, but you can also put a little magick into every preparation you make. Here, you'll learn some easy spells to charge every aspect of your entertaining from simple to elaborate, with extra "oomph" that will keep people looking forward to coming to your place over and over again.

ELEMENTAL CHARM

Use this spell to give yourself strength to cope with any "kerfuffles" that may erupt between guests at a party, or with any little accidents. Friendship is more important than a broken wine glass or a stained carpet.

∞

*Sun above and Earth below;**

Water rock me, cleansing Wind blow.

Inner strength, on with the show!

*For a night-time party, you could say "Moon above and Earth below."

BE STRONG SPELL

Use this spell when you discover that someone at your event is behaving offensively, or even if you just anticipate that it might happen.

∞

Nobody likes to be the baddie,

But no boorish lass or laddie

Is going to make my party saddy!

So I'll ask 'em to leave without getting maddy.

Trouble and its makers I command to be gone

With grace, and tactfully, I am strong.

GROUNDING

It can be hard to tell guests that they are making themselves unwelcome in your home because most people are brought up to avoid such confrontation. But it's okay to ground yourself and be reminded that it's reasonable to expect guests to follow your house rules.

Take a deep, slow breath—in through the nose, out through the mouth. Feel the floor beneath your feet. Notice that it's solid. Take another deep breath, and as you exhale, put your shoulders back and stand up straight. Think:

∞

It's my role, and I have the authority

To keep things as they ought to be.

It may be tough, but I am tougher,

And I'll use tact to be my buffer.

Manners Magick

Many consider the rules of etiquette to be a form of spell. Most people know to "see what fork the hostess uses," literally or figuratively, when they're not sure what to do in a social situation. And, as the host/ess, we guide other people's behavior with our own, a form of "sympathetic magick." Sympathetic magick involves acting out symbolically what you would like to see happen in the wider world. One example of the way this works is how you may touch the side of your mouth to show a friend that he has a crumb on the side of *his* mouth. Do you see how you already do the mechanics of magick every day? All you need to do to make it work even better is to *know* that you're working magick.

NO LONGER NERVOUS

This spell will help you calm down before hosting your party:

∞

By the power of Fire and Earth and Air

I will succeed as far as I dare.

I won't sweat it: Salt Water's the sea,

Bringing me passion and empathy.

As you recite the first line of this spell, touch both hands to your heart for Fire, then touch each hand to the opposite shoulder for Earth, and then open your arms and wiggle your fingers for Air. As you say the third line, make a brow-wiping gesture, as if you've been sweating, that's the Salt Water. Doing these things as you speak the spell invokes the Elements through your body. With the powers of Nature supporting you, you're free to consider other people's feelings, and make your party one everybody can enjoy.

Setting the Mood

With these spells under your belt for handling a simple visit, or the "big things" that can derail a party, you can now turn your attention to the details. There are lots of ways to enchant a party, whether it's dinner for two, an open house for twenty, or anything in between.

MAGICK PARTY FAVORS

Sometimes hosts and hostesses set out favors for guests to take home; guests can take them, leave them, or fiddle with them when they're sitting down for a few minutes. Here's a spell to make sure the party favors are charming, and not *just* silly. For this spell, you need:

* a small bowl of water
* a little bit of salt (on a plate or napkin is fine)
* a little bit of sugar (also on a plate or napkin)

Set the favors out on a table or other workspace. It doesn't matter whether they're lined up neatly or piled up, but they should be out of their packaging. Dip all ten fingertips in the bowl of water. Starting with your left pinky and the salt, alternate dipping your fingertips in salt and sugar. (Your left pinky should go into the salt, your left ring finger should go into the sugar, and so and so forth until your right pinky dips into the sugar.)

Hold your hands out, palms down, over the gathered party favors, and wiggle your fingers. The salt and sugar may stick to your wet fingers, but if some grains fall onto the favors, that's fine. As you wiggle your fingers, say the words of the spell, and be close enough to the favors that your breath touches them.

∞

With the Salt of the Earth and the sweet Fire of fun,

With Water and Air this spell is begun.

My guests will enjoy these jolly toys

They won't seem goofy; they'll seem groovy,

And this party will be a memorable one.

COZY CANDLELIGHT

If you're serving a candlelight dinner, you may want to put a spell on the candles. If it's a romantic candlelight dinner, you can begin by "anointing" the candles with a pleasant scent.

If you don't use perfume, you can use a paste made with water and household spices like cinnamon, rosemary, nutmeg, anise, or ginger; or maybe even cayenne to "heat things up" a little. When you're using a spice mixture, dab a little onto the bottom of the candle so that it won't leave a visible residue, and say:

∞

Earth in the spice, Fire in the glow,

Wine in the glass, Air in the flow.

Love be found as the candles burn down.

CONVIVIAL CANDLELIGHT

If your dinner is not amorous, you'll want to charm the candles a little differently. You can still anoint them with a pleasant scent—and if perfume or spices aren't feasible, then rub scented soap or lotion on them! To cast a "successful party" spell on your candles that will work whether they're tea lights, votives, tapers, or pillars, say:

∞

Candles burn cheery, candles burn bright,

Candles bring my guests delight!

Candles bring success tonight!*

*If it's a daytime party, you can change the last line to: *Candles bring success to light*.

Flower Spells

Flowers can be used in many ways, and add a lot to a party atmosphere. You can learn how to set a particular mood with flowers from many of books and Web sites, but have you ever thought about putting a spell on the flowers themselves? Here are a few that you can use. Select the one that's most appropriate for the sort of flowers you're using. Remember that you can substitute the word "event" or something more specific like "wedding" or "birthday" for the word "party" in any of these. As you say any of these spells over the flowers you're using, sprinkle them—even silk ones—with just a little bit of water. Water brings nourishment to flowers, and will carry the magick to them as well.

FORTUNATE FLOWER SPELL

∽

Scent of rose, cheer of daisy

Energy for this party raisy!

Curve of petal, shape of leaf,

Keep this party safe from grief.

WREATHY "WOO-WOO"

∽

Garland swagging 'cross the wall,

Make this the happiest party of all.

FLORAL TRIUMPH

∽

In flowers sweet, their colors bold,

Grace and beauty we behold.

Now increase our joy ten-fold!

CORSAGE CONJURATION

∽

Corsage to pin, energy spin

The power of a lovely time herein!

PLACE-SETTING PETAL MAGICK

∽

Little flowers at each place

Mundane cares and stress erase.

Petals and scent our joy enable;

Let pleasure blossom at this table.

Potions for Parties and More

Cocktail parties are back in fashion again and, while some people don't drink alcohol, this is good news. Cocktail parties are about friendship and conversation, and they're delightful opportunities to dress up and enjoy an adult, intellectual atmosphere that is too seldom part of our lives.

MAGICK³ (CUBED!)

Let's look at one of the basics of a cocktail party: ice cubes and crushed ice. Lots of drinks, hard and soft, are served "on the rocks" or over crushed ice and there's no reason for that ice to be ordinary. Here's a spell to enchant the ice cubes (whether you're going to use them as they come out of the tray or crush them) for your drinks. Say it as you put the ice tray in the freezer.

∞

Ice, cool our drinks and cool let us be,

But don't ice our per-son-alities.

Sparkling ice in glasses clink

So we all enjoy what we have to drink.

Ice, melt timely and dilute

So no one is a drunken patoot!

Air in bubbles and Earth in form

Fire make sure it won't get warm,

Water freeze — and do no harm!

As I will, so mote it chill!

You've probably noticed that ice cube trays can feature many shapes. You can make star-shaped ice "cubes," and ones shaped like shish kebobs! I've recently seen ones shaped like cats and dogs, too. If you use special ice cubes at your parties, other people's pleasure and amusement at seeing them will enhance whatever spell you put on the ice in the first place.

MAGICK UMBRELLAS

Not very many of us serve drinks with little paper umbrellas these days, but they're still appropriate for some theme parties. In case you throw one of them, here is a quick spell you can use on the umbrellas:

∞

Cute little 'brellas, make my guests laugh,

But do not choke them as they quaff.

Encourage mirth and let merriment accrue,

And if anything tears, let it be you!

Open and close, up and down,

With harm to none, and to no one a frown.

OLIVE SPELLS

Martinis and their cousins, Cosmopolitans, are popular now. More importantly, martinis are often served with olive or cherry garnishes, which you can quite easily enchant. You can do this spell at home when you're serving these "potions" or at play when you may order one at a restaurant. As you say this little spell, either out loud or to yourself, twirl the toothpick.

∞

What's oval and green, and full of red?

A stuffed olive, on a toothpick thread!

As [I] [we] [you] enjoy it, let it bring

Some happy hours of partying.

You can also say:

∞

Little olive that I bite,

Invite the magick that I need.

Bring me _____.

Let come no harm, and nothing impede.

CHERRY SPELLS

The cherry is usually found at the bottom of the glass, not on a toothpick, so you may not be able to twirl it the same way you can the olive. What you can do is lift your glass (perhaps making a wordless toast to your companions as you do) and very casually tap the side where the cherry's resting. That gesture, as well as twirling, will get its "magickal attention."

As you might guess, the Cherry Spell itself is different from the Olive Spell only in the first two lines:

∞

The cherry's sweet, and on a stem

It looks like a lucky gem!

As [I] [we] [you] enjoy it, let it bring

Some happy hours of partying.

You may want to work with this spell, too:

∞

Little cherry on a stem,

As I enjoy this little dram,

Work a magick strategem

That successful in my aim I am.

MINTY MAGICK

If you're making a mojito, you can charm the mint as you crush it. Mint is naturally refreshing, and can relieve nausea and cramping, making it the perfect ingredient for this spell!

∞

Mint so green, bright taste and smell

Ring this party like a bell!

And any tipsy trouble quell.

Colorful Drinks, Colorful Magick

Many party drinks are quite colorful, and colors themselves can have very positive magickal effects. Here are some color associations that you can relate to your favorite specialty drinks and some magickal toasts that you can use with any drink of that particular color.

RED

Red is associated with enthusiasm, passion, and determination, so use a red drink to enhance these qualities with this spell.

∞

Here's to all who've gathered here

With open hearts, to share good cheer.

Here's to all we're anticipating —

May we never tire of participating!

BLUE

Blue encourages calmness, patience, and relaxation, and will bring these qualities to the forefront
through this toast.

∞

Raise your glasses with me now,

And to this company allow

Me to make a toast and formal bow

'Cause I think you're all the cat's meow!

YELLOW

In magickal lore, yellow symbolizes energy, creativity, and intellectual pursuits, which are recognized in
this toast.

∞

I think we're not too tanked to think

That it's appropriate to thank

The folks with whom we're sharing drink

And on whose humor we can bank!

Here's to all of us and our

Minds and spirits — may they flower!

BROWN

The color brown represents groundedness, earthiness, loyalty, and reliability, which makes this appropriate to cola and coffee drinks.

∞

Should old acquaintance be forgot?

I think not!

May the roof above never fall in,

And we friends below never fall out;

And should we ever thirst,

May we save one another from drought!

CLEAR OR WHITE

In our Western culture, white stands for purity, honesty, and charity. This toast/spell incorporates those qualities.

∞

I raise my glass sincerely

And say to you quite clearly,

I love you all dearly —

Now let's go on being cheerly!

Clean It Up!

Here's a little something extra: a spell for the showers you'll be taking before you open the door to your guests, or head out for an evening on the town. It's not the sort of potion we've been talking about, but with this magick you are concocting a mix of shower water, sweat, grime, and psychic energy—a classic "witch's brew!" You're pouring this potion down the drain, where it can compost with all the other sewage, recycling nasty feelings.

SHIMMERING SHOWER

You can do this spell with nothing but the ordinary bath supplies you're already using, but if you want to get a special bar of soap, that's perfectly alright. You may also want to use candles instead of your regular bathroom lighting, but that too is optional.

In the shower, take a few seconds to appreciate the water flowing over your body, and imagine that it's a waterfall in a peaceful, private, and magickal grotto. Close your eyes and visualize the water glowing with a silvery light, and feel its touch as cleansing, refreshing and healing. Allow the warmth of the shower water to draw your worries and frustrations to the surface. Some of them will start to rinse away immediately!

Now lather up, and if you're washing your hair, save that for last. (If you normally wash your hair first, this change in routine will intensify the spell.) Starting with your face, gently wash every part of your body. In your mind's eye, "see" your troubles washing away.

If you are so inclined, sing a little. The important thing is to get lost in your lyrics so the soap and water really do wash you clean of everything that bothers you. If you're soulful enough, it won't even matter whether your words rhyme or not.

Here's a suggestion for lyrics, but feel free to make up your own.

∞

Oh, water . . . oh, oh water . . .

Oh, water, washing me!

Before you're down the drain,

I'll be rid of all my bane

I'll be clean, I'll be healthy, I'll be free!

When you wash your hair, you may want to sing a different song. A variation on "I'm Gonna Wash That Man Right Out of My Hair" from *South Pacific* may work for you. But if you're already into belting out the blues, just carry on! As you end your song, look down at the drain to see the shadows of your frustrations twisting down, down, into the sewer where they belong. When the water runs clear of soap, the spell's complete. Seal this spell by patting yourself dry with your towel, saying:

∞

Nice and clean and comfy dry,

No more frustrations can get by.

With harm to none I'm fortified,

And it is as I testify!

You can certainly use the Shimmering Shower spell to get ready for away-from-home activities, and you may find that some of the spells in the next chapter will be helpful at home, too.

·5·

SPELLS
FOR FUN
& FROLIC

Some adults believe that play is only for children, and many are even impatient for children to finish playing and attend to the more serious affairs of the moment. As a Wiccan priestess, one of my concerns is with balance, especially the balance of work and play in our lives. Indeed, the common wisdom in both medical and counseling fields these days is that play is as important for grownups as it is for children. A lot of social nuance is contained in adults' playfulness, and being unable to understand and participate in grown-up play limits a person's opportunities for social interaction.

It is true that adults need to balance their sense of being part of a group with being comfortable as an independent individual, and the capacity for play enriches every aspect of our lives, whether we're working or socializing with other people or spending time on our own. Yet it's also true that to be able to enjoy grown-up "play," we need to feel comfortable in a wide variety of social situations. So this chapter includes some spells and potions for use in many of those situations—and which you can share with your inner child.

Many of us need to teach our inner children how to play, and almost all of us need to rediscover appropriate ways to be playful as adults. Here are some ideas and spells to help you achieve both of these purposes.

Magick Picnics

We can understand "picnics" to be any meal we take in an informal setting—away from a table, indoors or out. Many of us remember tea parties with childhood dolls, sandwiches in a makeshift "fort" or hotdogs cooked at the hearth or over a campfire. We can call all of those occasions "picnics," and can't deny that many of them are remembered as magickal. Even as a grownup, you can have a picnic at home or away, inside or outside, day or night. If you don't have a basket to carry what you'll need, use a cardboard box or a paper bag. You can decorate the container. Baskets are more festive with a few ribbons tied or fake flowers tucked into their rims; paper bags can be drawn on with markers or crayons.

Whenever you're planning a picnic, you want to gather a few items—tablecloths, napkins, utensils, cups, etc.—together beforehand. As you pack what you'll need for your magickal picnic, you can enchant each "ingredient." Here are some spells to use.

TABLECLOTH SPELL

To enchant the tablecloth, spread it out on your table at home. Use the pointer and middle fingers of each hand to make little "people" who dance about on the cloth. If you're using a checkered cloth, have them hop from square to square. In a sing-songy voice, say:

With this cloth I censure

All misadventure

By color and texture

Good fun I conjure!

Now fold the cloth, corners to the center to make a square. If your cloth is round or rectangular, make some adjustments, but once you've made the square, say:

∞

Corner to center, and center will hold

Fun untold; the spell will work when the cloth unfolds!

Now you can fold the cloth up so that it will fit in your container, and put it in.

NAPKIN CHARM

Next, the napkins need to be charmed. Lay them out on the table, side by side and folded as you'll set them out on the tablecloth when you arrange your picnic. Stack them one on top of the other, while saying:

∞

With the spirit of play these napkins I bless:

Not to wipe out the fun, just to clean up the mess!

Now put them in your picnic container, too.

MAGICK UTENSILS

Depending on what food you take, and how you pack it, you may or may not need utensils, but it's better to have them and not need them than to need them and not have them, so here's how to enchant them to enhance your picnic.

∞

Knife and fork and spoon

Bring to my play this boon:

Morning, night or afternoon,

Serve up fun! This magick be done!

CHARMING PAPER CUPS

Whether you take paper cups, ceramic mugs, or plastic glasses, or a drink in a can or box or bottle, you'll want to be sure that it contributes more than mundane refreshment to your picnic meal. Here's a way to charm your drinking vessels. Hold each cup or glass up, as if you were toasting, and then to each side as if you were clinking glasses with people next to you. Then hold the glass or cup straight out in front of you, and say:

Cup be chalice, mug be drinking horn.

Let fun of imagination be born.

When with magick potion filled

Let unembarrassed play be distilled!

Now your cups or mugs are ready to go in your picnic "basket," and you're ready to plan your picnic menu.

FOOD SPELLS

When you decide what you want to eat on your picnic, here are spells to put on the food. Remember that spells can't keep your food safe to eat—wrap items carefully and use ice to keep them cool so you don't get food poisoning! Cast these spells as you're preparing or packing the food, whichever seems most appropriate to you.

Enchanted Veggies

This first spell will work on any form of vegetable, whether they're cut into individual servings or part of a salad. You can even use it with vegetable juice!

∞

Colorful vegetables, leaf and root

Make sure magick is afoot!

Nourish our senses, root and leaf,

And today suspend our disbelief!

Main Dish Mojo

To enchant your main dishes, all you have to do is look at them while you say the words below; but if you'd like to hold your hands (palm down) over them, or wiggle your fingers at them, that's fine too.

∞

Between the bread, between the worlds,

Let magick through our day unfurl.

Veggie, vegan, or with meat,

When we take a bite, it's fun we'll eat!

OR

∞

Casserole, pizza, shepherd's pie,

This main dish brings magick by.

Whatever we imagine, it can be

And we'll have fun accordingly!

If you're picnicking on your own you can change "we" and "our" to "I" and "my." Sometimes you have an inclination, or an opportunity, to be playful when there's no one around who can share the fun. When that happens, it's fine to indulge by yourself. If anyone asks for an explanation of your behavior, you can always say you're checking out a behavioral therapy technique—which will be perfectly true!

SWEET SPELLS

These two spells serve two different purposes. One is to help with a diet's success, and the other makes sure that the fun doesn't end just because the meal's concluding.

Moderation Magick

Your dessert needs a spell, too—and not one to keep the pounds off! You'll have to reach *that* goal by sensible mundane methods. But putting a spell on the process may help, so here's one to try.

∞

Three's the magick number on which I count

To keep my weight and calories to a reasonable amount.

I'll take no more than three bites

Of no more than two delights

On any one day,

And that's the way I'll count down

To a size that won't make me frown.

Dessert Fun Spells

This spell is to put the dessert to work maintaining the fun you're having.

∞

Fresh fruit from tree or vine

Keep things fun, not asinine!

Healthy and tropical or quite plain,

Keep our thoughts in amusing veins.

With this spell, you can make a favorite dessert support the fun of having this picnic, and set the stage for having more fun anytime you enjoy (or share) this particular sweet again, whether it's a cookie, a brownie, or a piece of pie or cake. The more often you make this spell part of your excursions into play, the more powerful it will become, until eventually it will let you find the fun in anything you're doing.

∞

Tastes of sweet to finish,

With you the fun's built-inish!

When next we taste you again,

A sense of fun we'll once more attain.

PICNIC POWER

When you have your gear in your basket, bag, or box, and the food's packed, you're ready to set a spell on the whole kit and endeavor. You may wonder if doing so is interfering with someone else's free will. I don't think so, because they'll still have the option of choosing to have a great or a terrible time. Basically, you're making an effort to show someone an especially good time, but you're not forcing their responses.

Don't worry if you're not using a picnic "basket." The word is symbolic of whatever's holding your fixin's. And don't worry that the rhymes aren't exact—that's part of the play! Hold or touch the basket, box, brown bag, or other container while you say these words:

∞

Picnic basket, picnic meal,

Help this day have great appeal.

Be a place and time to savor

And safe to indulge in play behavior!

By the power of our inner children,

Let this spell work unhindered.

Toys as Magickal Tools

Toys worked magick for us when we were kids, turning us into drivers and pilots, cowboys and ballerinas, pirates and anything else we could dream up. Now that we're grown up, some of us still have toys, and even if we don't play with them as we used to, they can still work magick for us by inspiring our sense of fun and creativity.

However, some toys are associated with established mythologies and magicks of their own; you don't have to enchant them. They'll cast a spell on you without you having to cast a spell on them first. For example, in my home office, I have a plush Smiley-face doll. When I press its tummy, it laughs like a little kid! There's definitely no need to further enchant that! I have other toys that are enchanted by personal associations and you probably do too. Maybe one is a teddy bear that can still cast a comfort spell! Here are a few examples of spells you can adapt to use with your own toys.

MISTAKES MAGICK SPELL

A ceramic pair of waltzing elephants commemorates one of my mistakes. While proofing a manuscript by reading it aloud, I saw "elephants on the Altar" instead of "Elements on the Altar." These elephants remind me that often, mistakes are inspirational, even if some of them need cleaning up after. No doubt you've made funny mistakes, too, and are reminded of them by something you have. If you don't already have a memento, you may be able to find, make, or draw something to represent a "goof" that was especially humorous. With this spell, instead of being embarrassed and trying to avoid the memory, you can use it to inspire creative fun.

∞

Goof up, screw up, tongue-tie, oops!

Let me giggle at my blooper!

Release the stress and I'll regroup

And not worry about what I need to scoop.

IMAGINATION MAGICK

We grownups can be self-conscious about playing, and feel uncomfortable having any of the trappings of childhood "silliness" nearby. But we're often too sentimental to get rid of our toys altogether. The next three spells help you draw on the energy of child's play to make your adult life *less* stressful and *more* productive.

∽

Silent [dollies] sitting there, *

You don't mind if I turn and stare.

The patterns that you show and hold

Give me ideas manifold.

*Substitute the name of one of your toys for "dollies" to personalize this spell.

TAKING A BREAK SPELL

Most adults don't play with their toys, but for many that's only true physically. Even though I no longer sit on the floor and move my toys, I *do* play with them in my mind when I need a refreshing break. These spells will help you use your toys to break up your day too!

∽

Toys and figures, make me smile;

Just for now, my thoughts beguile.

Be like a mental chamomile,

Distract me for a little while,

And then with work I'll reconcile.

MORE IMAGINATION MAGICK

∽

Happy trinket, do-se-do.

Help me make my thinking go.

Smiling and waving yourself around,

Help my thoughts get off the ground.

INSPIRATION MAGICK

Some of us deliberately keep a few toys where we can see them, maybe as a promise that when we finish our work, we'll have a chance to indulge a favorite hobby. You may know someone who collects and displays figures that relate to a particular television show or movie series, miniature animals of their favorite breed, or other collectibles—and maybe you do, too. Here's a way to use these things magickally.

∞

Eclectic collection, speak to me

And stimulate my mind.

Share with me your wild ideas:

*My [writer's] [working] block unbind!**

*When you say this spell, the last line may be "my ad campaign block unbind," or "my personnel decision block unbind," or "my schedule challenge block unbind." Maybe the idea you need is for your "transportation block" or your "confidence block."

Inner Play Spells

You might have a few toys—or playful accessories, like a leopard-print throw pillow or a retro kitty-clock—in your possession, too. You may be saving them for children or grandchildren, and maybe they're just souvenirs of a happy childhood, or happy moments. Do you want to help them help you to have more fun? Here are spells you can use on just about any toy or accessory.

TOY ENCHANTMENT I

For this spell, you need:

* the toy or accessory you want to work with
* a small, pretty stone
* a feather
* a candle
* a match
* a small dish of water

Put the stone and the candle in the water. If the candle won't stand by itself, drip a bit of wax into the bottom of the dry dish and stand the candle in the wax. Wait two or three minutes, and then put water in the dish again. Float the feather on the surface.

Set the toy on a table where there is room to put the bowl in front of it. Bring the bowl to the toy, as if you were bringing a birthday cake to the party table, and say—or sing—this spell:

∞

Little [toy] [thing], remember play,

And when I need, remind me:

When I get too serious

Or overly imperious,

Then, you must spellbind me,

That I may giggle, dance and smile,

And let my grownup rest a while,

And with my play-self reconcile.

Why does this spell work? Because you're essentially asking this object to open the door between your grown-up world and the childhood world of play. The bowl of water with the stone, the feather, and the candle is the gift that you bring when you're invited into someone else's home—in this case, the home of your inner child, represented by whatever article you've chosen.

Imagine that the candle is lighting your way to the Land of Play, which may be foreign to you now. You may imagine that the pretty rock is a precious gem, that the feather is from a magickal bird that can fly to other worlds, and that the water is the sea you can cross to find any land of legend that intrigues you. Realize that these gifts are precious, for to be allowed back into the Land of Play as an adult is a very special gift indeed, and worthy of something precious in return.

Keep this charmed item nearby and guard it as you would the key to any important doorway.

TOY ENCHANTMENT II

For this spell, you need:

* a very small toy
* a box (cardboard will do, but wooden is better) just big enough to hold it
* pretty cloth or wrapping paper to line the box
* scissors
* white glue
* a small bowl of water
* a serving of milk or juice and cookies or another snack
* decorations for the outside of the box (optional)

First, line the box with pretty cloth or wrapping paper. If you're using a wooden box, use your fingers to "paint" a 50/50 mixture of craft glue and water on the interior sides and bottom of the box, and apply pre-cut sections of cloth. If you're using cardboard, wrap the box and its lid separately with gift paper. If necessary, line the inside corners with cord or glitter glue, and let the box dry overnight. As you work, think of favorite childhood stories and games, and favorite pre-pubescent party and vacation memories. When any glue is dry, put the toy and the box side-by-side on a counter or table. Have a glass of milk and cookies or a similar snack handy. Dip your finger in the milk or juice and touch it to the toy. Break off a small bite of the snack and offer it to the toy, leaving just a bit of crumb behind. Then take a sip of milk and a bite of the cookie yourself. Say:

∞

Little toy, now we share

A little sip, a little bite

With your protection I will dare

To take, sometimes, a fancy-flight.

Little toy, I give to you

This wee housie, all prepared

And you, I know, will show me true

The play for which I've been impaired.

Set the toy in the box, and close the lid. Kiss the tip of your finger, and touch the lid. Whenever you feel you need a bit of fun, open the box and let the toy sit atop it while you have another glass of milk and a snack. When you do this, you'll soon find an opportunity to play—and if you take each such opportunity, another will always present itself.

Don't be alarmed or embarrassed if you start feeling like taking care of your toy, bringing it appropriate accessories. That's okay—in fact, it's great. It means the magick is working and you're learning how to play again. Good for you!

Charms for Social Success

One famous form of magick that we've talked about before is "glamoury," which lets you appear to other people the way you want them to see you. That's right! Putting on a style and colors that flatter and present you as you wish to be seen is a silent spell. And if you think "glamour" is about makeup and clothing, you're on the right track! However, it's not *all* about that. You can dress a person up in the finest clothes, and if s/he doesn't believe that s/he's as elegant or authoritative as s/he looks, s/he won't look elegant or authoritative. Instead, s/he'll look like s/he's playing dress-up—and expecting to get in trouble for it. Like all real magick, glamoury comes from the inside, but your clothes and grooming are among the tools you can use to work that particular magick.

LASTING GOOD LOOKS SPELL

Even when you know that your wardrobe is working for you, you sometimes want a little extra help. Here's one to use when you're combing your hair. It involves gestures in addition to the words you need to say, and those are in parentheses.

∞

Air for banter (laugh)

Fire for cheer (smile)

Water for the decanter (deep breath and relax)

Earth for the company of peers (click your heels together).

Every time you touch or readjust your hair, some of this spell's magick will be released, and your personal charm will be recharged.

MIRROR MAGICK

This spell will help you remember that you're a cool person and that, as Al Franken's *Saturday Night Live* character used to say, "doggone it, people like you." While standing in front of the mirror, trace your image with a moistened fingertip. Above the image, draw a star. Then draw rays—like rays of light to suggest that you are shining—around both the star and your image. Say:

∞

I am the charming hostless

Of this successful event.

My soirees offer the mostest

Of what makes guests content!

Now blink three times, and look again. See yourself really glowing with social charm.

HANKY CHARM

Unexpected company sometimes surprises us all, but if you have a few minutes' notice you can cast a spell to ensure your guests feel welcomed. Find a tissue or a cloth handkerchief and, in it, collect these items:

* a wee bit of dust
* a few grains of sugar
* a few grains of salt
* a few drops of perfume or cologne

If you don't have any cologne handy, scrape off a bit of scented soap or deodorant into the tissue or handkerchief. Fold the tissue's corners to the center, and then fold it twice more to make a small square.

The dust is to make you and your guests comfortable in your home. The sugar will sweeten your mood, or keep it sweet. The salt protects everyone—because you may not know what circumstances have motivated the sudden visit. And the scent reminds you of your natural elegance, so you can respond to this surprise with dignity and greet your guest with genuine affection, no matter what else is required. If you have a pocket, put your folded "hankie charm" inside. Otherwise, tuck it under a couch or chair cushion.

DANCE FOR THE COMPANY SPELL

If you don't have any advance warning and are opening the door to unexpected guests, here's a little spell-dance you can use. Practice it ahead of time so you'll be ready when the doorbell rings; you'll probably want to do it before you open the door.

Step quickly, with three steps, to one side and then tap your foot; repeat the same sequence in the other direction, or backwards as if you're opening the door. Step to the right with your right foot, then move your left foot next to your right. With your right foot, step again to the right. Then tap your left toe at the side of your right foot.

To return or back up, step to the left (or backwards) with your left foot, then move your right foot next to your left. Make one more step, to the left or backwards, with your left foot. Tap your right toe beside your left foot and then go back to moving normally.

This "spell" works by acknowledging that your normal routine has been interrupted—that's what stepping off to the right represents. You may have been thrown off-balance, but have caught yourself with those three quick steps. When you tap your left foot, you're turning things around so you're back in control. Then you take three quick steps, back the way you came, or back from the door so you can admit your guest. That's coming back to retake control over the situation. The final tap, of your right toe beside your left foot, sets the spell.

As soon as possible after you do this, go to your kitchen. Run the back of your left hand (your right hand, if you're left-handed) under the tap, and put just a dash of salt on your moistened hand. Say:

∞

Salt of the Earth, that's me.

In my house it's safe to be.

Comfort I offer, no matter the mess.

To my charisma I have full access.

Now you're ready to entertain, with no worries about losing your cool.

Magick Floats

Making an ice-cream float can make people recall the fun of youth very quickly! Whatever your ingredients and however you put your float together, here are three spells to use: one for the ice cream, one for the soda, and one for the straw! Say the ice cream spell while you're scooping it into the glass. Say the soda spell while you're pouring it. And say the straw spell as you roll it between your hands before using it, as you bend the top part (if it's a bendy straw), or as you lower it slowly into the glass. Finish all of these spells by taking a sip of your float (or eating a bit of ice cream off the bottom of the straw) and saying "Mmm, mmm, mmm!" This will bring the power of the magick number three to your spell.

WE ALL SCREAM SPELL

∞

I scream, you scream, we all scream for ice cream

Right now we don't care if it broadens our beams!

We'll enjoy our floats, pure fun promote

And shout "oh boy!" in a good mood supreme!

ICE CREAM ALCHEMY

∞

Bubble, bubble — no toil, no trouble!

Brush the day's cares to piles of rubble!

Soda down the side of the glass

And no carbonation, and no adult affiliation

Is gonna make us say "Alas!"

EX-STRAW-DINARY SPELL

It's usually not good when something sucks,

But sucking this straw will bring me luck.

As the bubbles rise to my tongue,

I will feel glor-i-ously young

And my sense of play will come unstuck.

Carbonated Enchantments

Lots of drinks, hard or soft, are carbonated. Bubbles are fun, and they'll tickle even the most dignified sophisticate's nose. That's what makes them more fun than "still" drinks. Making it fun always makes magick stronger. Here are spells to use with what some people call "sparkling" drinks; both of them lend power to your goals.

BEGUILING BUBBLES

Tiny bubbles in my glass,

This, my dream, make come to pass.

_____ is what I want.

Bring it in your tickle piquant.

If you don't like the tickle of a sparkling drink, or if you don't feel it because you're using a straw, you can change the last two lines to:

∞

_____ is what I need.

Bring it as through my drink you speed.

CARBONATION CONJURATION

You might prefer to use this spell:

∞

Carbonation I'll not waste,

So as you bubbles burst and pop,

Work toward my goal of _____ post haste,

And let your blessings be nonstop!

Hocus-Pocus Holders

Lots of people use insulated drink holders to keep their hot or cold drinks at the right temperature, at a picnic or during a sports event. Here are two ways to charm your drink holders. The first will let the energy of the drink affect you, through the can or bottle, the holder and your hand even when you're not sipping from it. The second will let you continue to infuse the drink with the magickal powers you want it to have, right through the holder and the container. Both of these spells have seals built into them, too. As you slide your drink into the holder, say whichever spell is appropriate to your needs.

LIKE A GLOVE

Through terry or foam, drink-power won't roam,

It'll just come home . . . to me!

Into my hand, through the insulating band

As I command, so mote it be!

ALL IN HAND

Drink hot or cold, drink mellow or bold,

Do as you're told, and harken to me.

What you'll do is bring me bliss!

[Quality] you'll have as I hold, so mote it be!

Most of us look forward to holidays as part of the fun that we enjoy, but most of us also find at least some holidays a little bit stressful, too. The spells in the next chapter will help you reclaim the delight, and be more appreciative of the deeper meaning that many holidays hold.

·6·

HELP FOR
HOLIDAY
HASSLES

No matter how much you look forward to and enjoy a holiday or get-together, if it involves a gathering of family and friends, it's probably going to be stressful. Thankfully, there are many magickal ways to ease the stress of these occasions. Some of the magick is the kind you can share without worrying about alarming or offending anyone, and some is the kind you do on your own, without anyone else ever needing to know about it.

During the holidays it's important to pay special attention to the ethics of magick, and not to impose on anyone else's free will with any magick you do. It's fine, advisable even, to set your limits and make sure nobody pressures you into doing more than you're comfortable doing. It's not okay to pressure other people, magickally or otherwise, to do anything that makes them ill at ease. Doing this is not only wrong, but is disrespectful, both of other people and of the "holy" in "holiday."

Thanksgiving

At Thanksgiving, we give thanks for friends, family, and the prosperity and good fortune that we enjoy or look forward to. Many families go around the dinner table and have each person mention one or two of the personal blessings he or she is counting. If yours is one of those families, maybe you'll be the only member to understand that acknowledging the successes and lucky breaks in your life is a magickal act in and of itself.

INCREASED BLESSINGS

Counting a situation or event as a blessing affirms that you're happy it's part of your life, and this acknowledgement works as a form of sympathetic magick. By describing the good things that have already happened, you attract more good things. You also train your subconscious mind to look for the positive aspects of anything that happens, which works as sympathetic magick too. What you look for, you're likely to find! When it's your turn to speak, share your blessing, then say, "This is only one of the gifts that enhances my life. I know that next year I'll have more to share with you."

TURKEY SPELL

To cast this Thanksgiving spell, you need a turkey-shaped candle, which you can find at some drug stores, specialty candle stores, dollar stores, or even some grocery stores. You can enchant your candle as soon as you get it home, or wait until you're ready to set it on the table. To cast the spell sprinkle a little bit of nutmeg over the candle, and say:

∞

The only turkey at the table

Will be the one we eat.

Everyone will be polite

And the mood be sweet.

We'll all be gracious; we won't fight —

This Thanksgiving will be just right.

If you notice anyone beginning to behave badly, take that person aside and let him or her know how much you appreciate your guests setting an example of camaraderie. If a troublemaker is persistent, lead them to the door and tell them you look forward to having them over again when they can control themselves.

Remember, even if your turkey spell isn't working on your guest, it's working to help you handle the situation without being a turkey yourself. If that happens, it's not because the spell was inadequate but because the individual in question is so self-absorbed that s/he isn't aware of anything but his or her own agenda. Taking this person out of the mix is well within your rights as host/ess, and is, in fact, part of the way the turkey spell works to keep your Thanksgiving dinner harmonious.

But don't worry—if you set an example of not being drawn into any antagonistic games, your guests are likely to relax and enjoy themselves.

THE REST IS GRAVY

Do you use a gravy boat, creamer, or just a bowl and ladle? No matter what you serve your gravy in, you can use this spell to ensure a happy holiday. Before you fill the boat or bowl with gravy, dab just a bit of cooking oil on the bottom (inside) of the container, and say:

∞

Gravy, moisten up the meal.

Gravy, enmity conceal.

Gravy, all hurt feelings heal.

Gravy, happy time now seal.

Another way to use this charm, or to strengthen it, is to write these words on the back of a paper doily, and then affix the doily, with double-stick tape, to the saucer on which you set the gravy container.

Additionally, you can use this spell with any of the other dishes you're serving—potatoes, veggies, and even desserts.

Christmas or Yule

For Wiccans, the mid-Winter holiday is Yule, the Winter Solstice. Yule is sacred because, from this astronomical moment onward until mid-Summer, the days get longer and the Sun gets warmer, which is essential to continued life. Many Christmas customs are similar to Yule traditions, and that includes the enchantments you can use to ensure a peaceful, happy gathering.

ORNAMENT CHARMS

For this season's magick, keep a box of plain glass ornaments on hand. They're inexpensive, come in just about any color, and make great and unobtrusive charms. You can hang them on the tree or in other decorations—or somewhere no one else will see them.

All you really need, besides the ornaments themselves, are some markers. However, you may want to use pictures cut from magazines, fabric ribbons or flowers, sequins, and other such decorations. If you want to use these sorts of things, you'll need craft glue and scissors. On the ornament, you can draw pictures or symbols, or make them from craft materials.

✳ You can draw a representation of something you want to bring into your life. If you do this on a silver ball, it will add the symbolic magickal power of a full Moon to your secret magick.

* You can draw a representation of something you want to avoid in your life or at your celebrations. Draw it on a dark-colored ball to invoke the power of the waning Moon.
* You can illustrate a mood you'd like to create, on more than one ornament. Put one in each room, or hang several on your holiday tree.

You can also do this with other people. Decorating ornaments is a fun project you can share with family and friends. If they don't want to do magick, that's fine; they don't even have to know that you're doing it.

MAGICK FAIRY DECORATIONS

You can make magick fairy decorations with facial tissues, tissue paper, paper napkins, or cloth hankies or bandanas. If you have color choices, they can coordinate with the colors you associate with the purpose of your magick. See Appendix B to figure out what colors work for you. To make these fairies, you'll need:

* round-headed clothespins
* a circle of tissue or paper or cloth with a diameter that is a little more than twice the length of the clothespin (Most round-headed clothespins are 4" long, so a circle diameter of 8½" should work.)
* a small rubber band, a bread-tie, or a bit of string or narrow ribbon to tie the cloth around the "neck" of the clothespin doll
* a marker

Lay the clothespin with its "head" in the center of the circle and its "feet" at the edge. Fold the cloth over, and tie it at the clothespin's "neck," and voilà! You have a fairy doll! Use a marker (either in a contrasting color or in one that will blend in) to write the words of a spell on the inside of the skirt. Here are spells to use with them:

Peace Spell

∞

Christmas [Yuletide] fairy, bring me peace.

My stress decrease, my joy increase,

So I know Christmas [Yuletide] as I should,

In faith and grace and brotherhood.

Joy Spell I

∞

Fairy of wild joy, linger here!

I don't need to shed a tear.

All too soon it'll all be done —

Let it be with harm to none.

Joy Spell II

∞

Fairy of laughter, fairy of song,

Keep me happy and keep me strong.

Little fairy, don't let me pout.

Let me enjoy these days, throughout.

FESTIVE BREW

Brews can also be festive and often help infuse a celebration with just the right feelings of glamour or camaraderie. "Festive Brew" is the name of the drink that we serve at our Yule open house. As you stir the ingredients of your choice, say something like:

∞

Friendship's hot and weather's cool

Let this day shine like a jewel!

Without fail this spell adds sparkle to the gathering.

New Year's Eve

On the secular calendar, New Year's Eve ends the old year and New Year's Day begins a new one. This is a great time to use the energy of parties to magickally strengthen friendships. Here are spells to help you.

THE MAGICK OF FRIENDSHIP

Many people sing "Auld Lang Syne" on New Year's Eve and this singing can be thought of to be a spell in and of itself—a spell that bonds your friendships and includes newcomers in your hospitality. For your New Year's party, print the words on a big poster board, with room for everyone to trace their hands and sign their names every year. After a few parties, you might like to frame the poster board so the magick of your camaraderie can keep working for years to come. You may have to insist that your guests sing at least the chorus one more time, because, while one or two flat notes in the song won't do any harm, you don't want to release a *totally* discordant spell!

NO DRUNK SKUNKS SPELL

Are we just blessed with friends who know their drinking limit, do we all end up dancing the intoxication off . . . or does this spell have something to do with it? It's not subtle, but it's more subtle than throwing up! To help guarantee that your party guests won't get sick, use this spell on the bottles you provide and, once your guests arrive, keep an unobtrusive eye on consumption.

∞

Mixed or whiskey, beer or wine

As you go down, taste just fine

But don't come back up: wait your turn,

Till off to the potty our friends adjourn.

DANCE TILL DAWN

If your New Year's Eve bash—or any other gala—is a dance party, here are some spells you can use to ensure that a good time is had by all. Use them before your guests arrive, or before the dancing starts.

The Dance Floor Charm

∞

Floor, hold dancers moving left and dancers moving right,

Floor, support them to and fro and swaying through the night!

Feel their steps in friendship's name

And let it be to lasting acclaim!

The Music Charm

∞

Waltz and tango, fast or slow,

Release all inhibitions.

In celebration be steadfast

And merry keep tradition!

HOSPITABLE SAFE HOME SPELL

Every now and again, a guest has too much to drink. If you dread dealing with this, here's a spell to cast on *yourself* before your guests arrive. If there's a particular guest who is likely to overdo it, repeat the spell as soon as possible after that person arrives. (You can also privately let that guest know that you'll be looking out for him or her.) You need two things:

* a safe place to put a guest's car keys
* the number of a cab company, preferably on speed dial

Stand in front of a mirror to cast this spell and, smiling the whole time, make the motions of leading a guest back into the house, away from the door, and taking the car keys out of his or her hand. Say:

∞

If anybody has too much

Wine or beer or brandy,

Their keys I will not let them touch;

And I have a taxi's number handy!

For harm to none

Is why this is done!

Easter

The Wiccan Spring holiday is Ostara, which celebrates the return of light and life to the Earth in flowers and baby animals. These animals aren't just puppies, kittens, and peeping chicks, they're the fawns, cubs, and other animals that may, in a couple of years, die to the hunt so our families can live. Ostara is also a time to consecrate the fields and sanctify the seeds that will grow into the crops that sustain us.

For Christians, Easter is an equally sacred time, and the secular culture, too, enjoys egg hunts, and Easter baskets filled with chocolate bunnies and other toys. However, for many Easter dinner can be stressful, and entertaining with the "good china" can trigger some anxieties, too. Here are some spells to help you cope.

KEEP IT CLEAN SPELL

When I was growing up, my aunt was in charge of Easter dinners. She set a very fancy table: white cloth, gleaming silver, sparkling wine glasses, not to mention centerpieces she arranged herself, using flowers cut from her own garden. I don't think she literally enchanted her table, but you can certainly put a little spell on yours. "Keeping it clean" refers not only to the tablecloth, but also to everyone's interactions. This spell doesn't impose on other people's free will, it just sets your limits. After all, your house, your rules!

∞

Tablecloth smooth and spotless,

And every lovely frill,

Let no one be thoughtless:

No wine or meanness spill!

UTENSIL UTILITY CHARM

You can charm each place setting, too.

∞

Dinner plate, salad plate,

Fork, knife, and spoon,

Let us eat in peace

This afternoon.

Bowl and napkin,

Sparkling glass,

Let our behavior be first class.

Serving spoon and serving dish,

Let nothing here be devilish.

With health to all, let it befall.

FIERY FAITH BLESSING SPELL

Many families serve ham at Easter and even if you don't prepare it yourself, you can always make a little dish of maple and mustard sauce to complement its flavor. For this magickal recipe, you need:

* ½ cup mustard
* ¼ cup pure maple syrup

Maple and mustard are both "Fire" tastes, so to be sure you spark the right kind of fire at your table, use this spell as you mix them together:

∞

Maple and mustard, tree and seed,

Bring us the inspiration we need.

Faith and family, both are blessings —

Remind us of that as we taste this dressing.

When you put the bowl of maple-mustard sauce on the table, whisper "faith and family" over it, and the spell will be reactivated. You can make this sauce a day ahead of time and keep it chilled till you're ready to use it.

HOME IS WHERE THE HEART IS

Oftentimes, people are at their most nervous just as they open the door to welcome family into their homes. This can be especially true if you anticipate friction between guests. Take a moment for a calming breath before you answer the door, and say:

∞

Easter's [Ostara's] a time to rise above

And focus on a family's love.

I will glow with faith and trust

And not let my composure be mussed.

If there is trouble, I'll make sure

To guide us back to cheerier.

When we eat, we'll all be grounded —

And remember why this day was founded.

No harm will come to others or me

From this spell for harmony.

Mother's Day

Mother's Day has developed into a family reunion day, and that means that several generations may gather on that afternoon to celebrate with dinner and to honor mothers and grandmothers with cards and gifts. Like most family occasions, Mother's Day can be both joyous and stressful. Here are spells to help you maintain your composure whether you're hosting or guesting—and whether your mother is living, or known to you, or not.

MERRY FOR MOTHER

Many people spend Mother's Day with their mom. Sometimes that means coping with family members with whom it's difficult to get along. On this important day, a spell to keep these relationships smooth can help.

∞

Merry for Mother I will be,

No matter if someone's goading me.

I won't retaliate and I won't whine:

That's the least I can do for this mother of mine.

In my relatives I will see

What Mother loves, like she loves me.

SPEAKING SPELL

Even if you get along well with your family, it can be hard to express your feeling of love. Here's a spell that may help:

∞

It's hard for me to put into words

How I feel, but it should be heard,

And so today, I'll be undeterred,

And let her know how I feel.

For though I'd like to think she knows,

It'll be more special if it shows.

I don't have to be verbose —

I just need to keep it real.

RECEIVING THE GIFT

Unfortunately, not everyone's mother is living and there are some who have never met their birthmothers, but nevertheless wish them well on Mother's Day. To remember and honor an absent mother, all you need is:

* a piece of paper, white or colored, OR a white paper doily, at least as big as your hand
* a pencil, pen, crayon, or marker in a favorite color(s)
* an envelope with a Mother's Day card, if you'd like

Trace either hand on the doily. Inside the outline of the pinky finger, write "I'm all grown up!" In the outline of the ring finger, write, "I love you." In the outline of the middle finger, write, "I nurture people." In the outline of the pointer finger, write, "I remember you." And in the outline of thumb, write, "I have learned from you." Even if you don't remember your mother from personal experience, you probably remember hearing one or two things about her or maybe all you remember is what you've imagined or dreamed about her. That's okay. It still counts.

Across the palm of the outlined hand, sign your name in your best handwriting. Fold your art and put it in the envelope. If you have a Mother's Day card, sign that as well. Put it under your pillow that night. Two days later, open the envelope, take the artwork out and, as you're looking at it, say:

∞

What a good [son] [daughter] this mother has!

No other child could hope to surpass.

This mother should be proud, and say "I love you" out loud,

And this kid should know that s/he's got class!

Father's Day

You can just about use the same spells and charms for Father's Day as for Mother's Day. Simply change the word "Mother" to "Father," and the word "her" to "him." However, instead of making a missing father a traced hand, follow the cultural cliché and make him a tie! You still need a piece of paper and something to write with, but instead of an envelope, use a piece of ribbon.

On the paper, draw the shape of a tied tie. Decorate your drawing with the five sentences listed for the fingers of the traced hand. When you are done, roll it up and tie it with the ribbon. Instead of putting it under your pillow, set it on your headboard or nightstand. Two days later, unroll it and receive it on your father's behalf, using the "Receiving the Gift" spell above, but changing the word "mother" to "father."

Fourth of July

Because the weather's usually fine at this time of year, many of us attend parades or outdoor parties to celebrate our country's birthday. But no matter the focus of the events, these spells will help you enjoy them.

OH SAY CAN YOU SEE

Religion and politics are two volatile subjects of conversation, so even a party for the Fourth of July has potential for argument. Here's a spell you can share to help everyone keep their cool. Use little cards, each with two lines of the spell on them, and set them out in a row so your guests read them as they enter the party.

Is this spell manipulative? I don't think so. I think it amounts to setting out the party rules, much as you might put up a sign that says RECYCLE HERE or PAPER PLATES IN THE TRASH, PLASTIC UTENSILS IN THE SINK. Each guest reads the series of signs silently to him- or herself as she passes them, and understands your expectations as a host.

∞

Oh say can you see how it ought to be?

*This country's yours and mine,
and together today everything can be fine!*

We'll celebrate and not excoriate,

And if it's not great we'll help create

The shared enthusiasm to avoid cataclysm.

We'll trust that we each want to heal the breach

*Even if we have diff'rent ideas
about how things should be to please us.*

Hip hip hooray for the freedom to say

"Happy Fourth of July!"

SPARKLER SPELLS

In states where sparklers are legal, you can put a spell on them, which will be released as they burn. Casting these spells is no more unethical than putting coasters out to protect your table from guests' glasses. It's a natural part of what hosts do to make parties successful. There are several spells here. Feel free to use whichever one you find most appropriate.

∞

Twinkle, sparkle, red, green, and gold

Our heritage is more than 200 years old!

It's been here a while and it's here to stay,

And we raise one voice in a "hip, hip, hurray!"

OR

∞

Sparkly colors, red, white, and blue,

Let us for our country do

What we think is best, what we think is right —

And let us start by respecting each other tonight!

OR

∞

In these sparklers' red glare

Let us see the reason

To let love burst in the air

In this freedom season.

Our hearts are aglow

With the dream that's still there.

No matter how each of us sees the potential,

Let love of liberty be our common credential.

RED, WHITE, AND BLUE SPELL, HOLD THE BLUES

Maybe you need a quick spell to ensure safety over the Fourth of July weekend. After all, you don't want trouble 'round the pool, ants at the picnic, or a sunburn! No problem! In fact, you can use this spell to make any summer party a success. All you need for this spell is one of the napkins you're setting out for the guests and a plastic fork. Unfold the napkin and hold it at the center, so the four points hang loosely. In your other hand, hold the plastic fork, tines pointing out and upward. Begin at the door where your guests will enter, and walk clockwise through all the spaces where your guests will circulate. Don't forget the bathroom!

As you go around the house, shake the napkin as though you're dusting away any possible dangers or annoyances, and poke with the fork. Repeat the following lines:

∞

Only fun, and only safety

No skin or grill shall be overdone

People, laugh but don't act daftly

Good vibes only, and harm to none.

GOOD FOOD SPELL

As you set out the tableware and the food (for the Fourth of July or any party!) say:

∞

Good food, food fun,

And easy clean-up!

No spilling, no illness;

Come off without a hiccup!

Halloween

Halloween is a special holiday for a lot of people. For Wiccans and other Witches and Pagans, Halloween is a religious holiday that marks the end of Summer as the final harvest. It's also a family reunion that includes loved ones who have died, and is the beginning of the Wiccan new year. Even if you're not Wiccan, Halloween is a great holiday! However, you may want to cast spells to ensure that your party goes off without a hitch.

HALLOWEEN PARTY SPELLS

Halloween is a great time to get together, dress up, and celebrate! Here are spells to bring success to your Halloween costume party. Again, they're perfectly ethical preparations for an enjoyable event, no more coercive than putting out guest towels in the bathroom.

∞

Have a good time, friendly folk,

In mask and makeup, hat and cloak.

Let us guess who you might be —

But please don't be too scare-y!

OR

∞

Trick or treat, play and party!

Let everyone be hale and hearty!

With sweet treats and clever tricks,

This party will be a successful schtick!

TRICK-OR-TREAT SPELLS

If your children are going trick-or-treating, make sure they're safe. Use face paint instead of masks so their vision isn't obscured, and incorporate reflective material into their costumes. And of course, ask them to bring their treats home before they eat them. If your children are younger than five, a grownup will go with them, but you may also put a protective spell on them even without their permission. If they're older, ask them if it's alright for you to put a good spell on them to help the evening go well. To cast this protection spell, say:

∞

Door to door and bell to bell,

Be protected by this spell

From ghosties and ghoulies and menace unseen,

And come home safe this Halloween.

OR

∞

In a nifty costume, with a ready sack,

Be tired and satisfied when you come back!

OR

∞

Dressed as something you think is cool,

Have a good time with the other heroes and ghouls.

Mind [name of supervising adult] and very careful be

And remember it's all make-believe.

OR

∞

Have a good time, and don't be scared:

My love is with you everywhere.

It's safe to go, and safe you'll come home

For good ghosts watch over you while you roam.

(If an older child says s/he'd rather you didn't cast a spell, invoke your parental prerogatives to go over the safety rules in a very mundane way, set a curfew, or even arrange for some unobtrusive adult supervision.)

Birthdays and Anniversaries

In one sense, birthdays are magickal all by themselves, because no matter how old we get on the outside, we usually feel younger on the inside. Thus, the first rule of magick applies to birthdays in this way: do not give anybody a surprise party unless you are absolutely sure they'll be *pleasantly* surprised.

The same goes for anniversaries. Not everyone has a wedding anniversary, but many of those who do like to be guided by either a traditional or modern list of correspondences, which I've included in Appendix E. Married or not, everyone has some milestones to mark, happy or bittersweet. The same list of gift correspondences can be used for any anniversary, from graduation to retirement!

At birthday and anniversary parties, there are several ways of working a bit of subtle magick to make the occasion run as smoothly as possible.

BIRTHDAY CAKE PLATE CHARMS

If you're the host, of course you want the event to go well, and charming the cake plate and knife will help. It doesn't matter whether these are special utensils, or just an ordinary plate and knife pressed into service. You can change these birthday charms to anniversary charms by changing a few words. To cast this spell, say:

∞

Round like the cake, and like seasons flow

Hold this dessert and the party safe

Until the candles [birthday person's name] does blow!

Then hold the crumbs and celebration

Safe and sound till culmination.

You can also use the following spell:

∞

Platter, hold this birthday cake

And not one crumb lose or forsake.

Hold us safe in celebration

Till this party's culmination.

WEDDING ANNIVERSARY PLATE CHARM

To cast this spell, say:

∞

Cake plate, as we celebrate

What once happened on this date,

And everything that's happened since then

That gives us joy again and again,

Do not let our pleasure abate,

And help this party be really great!

CAKE KNIFE CHARM

You can also cast a spell on the knife the couple is using to cut the cake. To cast this spell, say:

Cutting edge, just like our guest

Cut slices everyone likes best.

Keep the cutting to the cake,

That no errors on this day we make.

COLOR SPELLS

Most celebratory cakes have two features in common: decorations and candles. Quite often, both the decorations and the candles are schemed to acknowledge the birthday boy or girl's favorite colors or activities. Here are a few quick charms for both the candles and the cake's décor. You can use these charms with the candles alone, decoration alone, or even with sauce or garnish, if your "cake" is some other kind of dessert. Refer to Appendix B for additional color associations, and use them with cakes, other refreshments, table settings, and decorations to make your enchantments even stronger.

"Red"

∞

Red for the love we feel for our guest:

Let this [birthday] [anniversary] be the best

So far, with better still to come,

And may we long be pals and chums!

"Orange"

∞

Orange for the joy we share with our friend;

To this party our energy we lend.

So s/he may know how much we care,

We celebrate with orange flair!

"Yellow"

∞

Yellow's the color by which we show

How much [guest of honor's name] means to us.

Let all the shades of sunshine glow

As bright as our friendship does.

"Green"

∞

Green for growth and maturity:

Not getting older, just better, is s/he!

Green for soothing, green for calm,

And green for a day without a qualm!

"Blue"

Water bless blue, and sky bless it too;

And only mood should not be blue.

Blue means loyalty, that is true —

And this blue is for friendship entre nous. *

*entre nous is French for "between us."

"Purple"

Purple dark, purple light

Purple coloring just right,

I know you can, I say you will

This party and all of us with love and joy instill!

These spells will also work on wrapping paper, ribbon, other party decorations, and even on any colorful drinks you serve.

There's one other bit of birthday magick that just about everybody does, and most people feel is magickal— and that's singing "Happy Birthday." When you sing it, put your heart into it and mean it truly. It will be one spell of love and protection that you *can* do without formally asking permission.

Vacation

There are a lot of commercials for travel and transportation companies that poke fun at what can go wrong on a vacation, and lots that insist only *they* can make it special. If you'd rather not rely on any one advertiser to make your hard-earned trip the best it can be, there's certainly no harm in casting a few spells.

HOME SAFE HOME SPELL

This is a spell you can use whether you're going on a vacation or just to the store; everybody wants to get home without trouble and no one wants to deal with disturbance or disaster when they get there.

∞

As I leave and lock each door,

I lock in protection, roof to floor.

In every room and corridor,

Of every closet, cabinet, and drawer,

And of furnishings, so I am sure

That nothing will happen here before

I get home, and not then either:

Of safety and luck this charm's a bequeather!

LUGGAGE SPELL

With luggage rates going up, every bag can use all the help you can give! If you have a pen that's the same color as your luggage's lining, you may want to write these words right inside. You can also recite this spell as you fill out the information that goes on your luggage tag, or, if the tag's big enough, write the words on the back of it.

∞

Hard side, soft side, check or carry:

Be carefully handled, and nowhere tarry,

Except of course, where I shall go,

And then be with me, safe in tow.

Do not break, be burgled, or tear.

Be intact with my stuff when I get there.

GOOD TIMES SPELL

We've all heard stories of disastrous events plaguing a vacation. Here's a spell that will help keep those things from happening to you. Say this to your itinerary in a commanding voice, or write it over an extra copy of it:

∞

When I get there, there shall be

Weather just right for my [fam'ly][plans] and me.

Nothing untoward or scary will go down,

Nothing to make me weep or frown.

There'll be nothing with which I have to "cope,"

And nothing to make me sick, or mope.

To my return from my embarkation,

This will be a great vacation!

BUSINESS CLASS

Not all the traveling we have to do is on vacation. People also travel for business, financial reasons, or to visit family. Here's a spell to use for those trips:

∞

Very successful my trip will be.

Nothing will fall out from under me,

And only and all best outcomes I'll see.

Everything will work out, nice and neat,

And I'll come safe home with my mission complete.

At least now and then, we all get the feeling that we're always on the move—our lives these days can be "go, go, go." We can anticipate some events, but there are bound to be some surprises, too. We need to be able to think on our feet and make our own magick no matter where we are, night or day. In the next chapter, you'll learn some ways of creating your own spells for use whenever and wherever you need them.

·7·

MAKE YOUR OWN MAGICK, ANYTIME, ANYWHERE

We've all seen movies featuring wizards and witches who can cast spells at a moment's notice, for convenience or in need. Reading this book, you've learned that minus the special effects, anyone can do the magicks on these pages. But you may not have time to find the spell you want, and you may need magick that's more specific to your circumstance than any of these spells, charms, or brews. That's why it's important to be prepared. Read on!

Anytime, Anywhere

You're not always at home or at work when the need for magick arises. Throughout this book I've shown you some spells that work in various places and at various times, but here we'll concentrate on those that you can use at a moment's notice, or even during a crisis.

ENCHANTED POCKET TISSUES

Here's a spell that will help you keep your cool and focus your energy and attention appropriately, whether the need is expected or not. Most people carry—or at least mean to carry—a pocket pack of tissues with them at all times. Why not enchant those tissues to help you out of a sticky situation? Here are two spells to use, and if you need them to be multipurpose, you can cast both spells on the same packet of tissues!

∞

By the Earth in the tree you're made from

By the Fire of the sun's bright glance;

By the Water of tears you wipe away

By the Air that I sneeze, perchance . . .

The tissues that I carry with me

Will ever my magick advance.

Power rise as I pull from the pack,

And my use release the spell,

My need be met, no harm beget

And all distress be quelled.

When you need to, take out one of the pocket tissues and use it a bit dramatically—perhaps dabbing sweat from your brow—while saying:

∽

I'm not gonna lose it, whatever the issue —

'Cause I am using my magickal tissue!

A, E, I, O, AND U MAGICK

Eastern religions have taught us that we can control our body's response to stress by concentrating on our breathing and, though not all of us are skilled at this, it's becoming a familiar concept. Anyone can use rhythmic breathing to work a little magick without anyone else being any the wiser.

For this spell, as we exhale, we can very subtly and silently mouth one of the vowel sounds to activate spells you may not be able to say aloud. In some circumstances, it's alright if the sounds are at least a little bit audible, too. "Ahhhh" and "ohhhhh" and "ooooh" are expressions of enjoyment or appreciation, and they can all mean surprise, too. "Eeee" and "ayyyyy" (pronounce it "eye" and hold the sound) can indicate alarm or anxiety. Working with those Western cultural standards, here are a few spells you can memorize and use whenever you need them. Just remembering the purpose of the spell, even if you have forgotten the exact words, can work, too.

You might use one of these A, E, I, O, U spells when you're enjoying a fine meal, closing an important contract, meeting someone who interests you, having a great time playing with your puppy, doing better at an interview than you thought you might, experiencing an exercise high, or being confronted with any unexpected circumstance.

"A"

Ahhhhh, this is good; ahhhh, this is fine!

Let this success always be mine!

"E"

Eeeee, I don't like this! I want it to cease

And with this breath, it shall release.

OR

Eeeee-minie, creeminie, do-wack-a-do!

I'll breathe magick and make the best come true!

"I"

∽

Ayyyyy don't know what will happen next

But whatever it is, I won't be vexed.

OR

∽

Ayyyy'm not sure what I should do,

But I won't let that be my Waterloo.

"O"

∽

Ohhhh my goodness, golly whiz!

I'll take it in stride, whatever it is!

"U"

∽

Ooooh, I like this! It's unsurpassed.

I'll do what I can to make it last.

Condensed Magick

In most situations, most of us can move a hand or a foot without attracting too much attention. Intent is most of any magick, and our spells, charms, and brews are ways of focusing our intent. Therefore, when we need to, we can concentrate a big purpose into a little spell or charm—or movement. Here are some ways to do this kind of condensed magick.

CONVERSATION STOPPER

If you want a conversation to end, tap your left foot once. Then, keeping your heel on the ground, arch your foot over the spot you just tapped. Tapping the ground or floor lets the spot beneath your foot represent the conversation, and arching your foot *over* it symbolizes your desire for the chat to be over. When you swing your foot from left to right, it lets the conversation be complete when it ends. If you lift your foot straight up and only move it to the right or left, the end of the conversation will be more abrupt.

You can do the same thing with your hand. Using your left hand, touch the middle finger to your thumb. Then flex each finger of that hand individually, starting with your pinky, as if you were drumming your fingers on a tabletop. End by bringing your middle finger and your thumb together again.

If more than one person is involved in the conversation that you want to end, either repeat the gesture with your right foot (again moving it from left to right over the spot you've tapped), or shake your left hand as if to relieve a cramp. Then smile and excuse yourself.

RESCUE FLAIR

At one time or another, everybody finds themselves in an unpleasant situation that they need help getting out of. While you should rely on other methods if you're involved in a violent or dangerous situation, this spell works to turn you into your own rescuer. The other way it works is by psychically drawing attention to your circumstances, so that other people will be interested and be inclined to investigate or intervene.

So what do you need to do?

1. Take a moment to breathe deeply and give yourself enough space to stretch your arms in front of you and to your side. What you're going to do is build a psychic beacon to give whoever's troubling you pause, and to alert potential allies to your plight.

2. Close your eyes (unless that would put you in any physical danger) and take three deep breaths: in through your nose, out through your mouth. (It's alright to trigger one of the A, E, I, O, U spells when you do this, too.)

3. As you take the first deep breath, put your hands in front of you with your palms facing outwards and lace your fingers together. Stretch your arms forward, and visualize both a flashing red light and a "wee-ooop, wee-ooop" alarm sound emanating from your palms.

4. As you take the second deep breath, raise your arms over your head. Keep imagining the alarms going off.

5. As you take the third deep breath, unfasten your fingers and lower your arms to your sides, drawing a semi-circle with your outward-facing palms. Don't let the intensity of your psychic alarm fade at all.

6. When your hands reach your sides, you can silence the psychic "wee-ooop," but keep the psychic beacon flashing. Be alert to your surroundings so that you can make eye contact with anyone who seems curious, and do whatever else you can to encourage their approach.

This will work best if you send your psychic alarm with a great sense of purpose and authority, much as you would be assertive about letting people know about a fire in the building. If you're far from other people or in a great milling crowd, or if people's attention is tightly focused on other things, you may need to sound the alarm more than once. It's possible that the person who's causing your problems may wonder what on earth you're doing. Should you feel you need to offer an explanation, just say, "This is taking a lot out of me!"

REPLENISHING ENERGY

Sending out psychic alarms isn't the only thing that can tire you. Working hard, playing hard, preparing for a party, finding time for errands, helping a friend—all those things and more can run you ragged. The good news is that no matter where you are, you can revitalize yourself, and it's fairly easy to do.

Wiccans call this magick "grounding and centering," and it works by reconnecting you to humanity's greatest source of energy—the Earth itself. You will need at least one uninterrupted minute (take longer if you have more time), but you don't need any special materials to do this energy work. However, if you'd like to store a little extra energy in a talisman, you can hold a polished rock, key, or any other token you can keep handy while you do this. Some of the energy you raise will pass from your hand into the item you've chosen. Then later, you can hold it for an even quicker pick-me-up! Next:

1. Sit or stand somewhere comfortable and safe. It's best if you can see the sky from the place

you've selected, but it's not absolutely necessary. Do know what the weather is when you're working, though.

2. Put your feet flat on the floor. Visualize the concrete or plywood beneath the carpet and, beneath all the construction material (including any other floors of the building you're in, or the floor of the vehicle that's carrying you), the ground. Imagine dark, rich, fertile soil. Imagine you can feel this wonderful dirt between your toes. Imagine its temperature. Feel your toes wiggle. Feel the Earth supporting you, steadying you.

3. Breathe in, deeply, through your nose. Notice that the same comfort your toes are feeling in the dirt is rising up through your calves and your hips, along your back, and into your shoulders and neck. You feel strong. As you realize this, exhale slowly, through your mouth. Ahhhhh. (Yes, feel free to release the power of the "Ahhhh" spell here.)

4. Take another deep breath. Feel the power of the Earth, gentle but firm, coursing through your veins. Feel it strengthening your legs and arms. Roll your neck and flex your shoulders. As you straighten your spine, feel the relaxed power of the Earth refreshing you.

5. On your third deep breath, imagine yourself cocooned in a ball of pale blue-green light. This light will seal in the Earth's power, making it available for you to use for the next few hours. If you are storing some of this energy in a talisman, visualize it wrapped in the same blue-green light.

When you turn your attention back to whatever you were doing before you took this re-energizing break, your mind should be clear and you should be ready to take it all on again. If you do this exercise daily, and sometimes give yourself the opportunity to take longer than one or two minutes, you'll find that your overall energy levels will increase, as will your enthusiasm for everything you do.

Making Your Own Magick

If you take a moment to think about it, it's not hard to understand that we are all magickal beings. The ideas that you have are unique. The way you do any of the magick in this book is different, even if only a little bit, from the way I've done it, and that gives your magick its own special strength. However, although you and I do our magick for different goals and with our own unique flair, we're still using the same basic techniques. We're like children building different castles with identical sets of blocks—a good example, because our inner children give our magick its energy, and the magick we do helps turn our lives into the castles we inhabit and makes our own special "fairy tales" come true.

You've got several charms, chants, brews, and other magicks at your disposal now, but there might be times when you need or want to compose your own. Can you do that? Yes, you can. Magick is natural and is just as legitimate for us to use in our lives as any other skill, and provided that we stay within our moral parameters, the magicks we create for ourselves are the best ones for our lives.

As you know, there are various types of spells, and most of them are a combination of several elements: written and/or spoken words, physical materials, and your *own* need and intention. Let's look at each of those elements in turn.

WRITTEN AND/OR SPOKEN WORDS

Very often, the words to a spell are rhymed. I'm sure you remember this one from childhood:

∞

Rain, rain, go away!

Come again another day.

You probably have examples of nonrhyming spells in your kitchen, too—in your cookbooks! Recipes are spells of a sort: they use written words to combine ingredients to achieve a very specific goal, like a particular dish for breakfast, lunch, or dinner. In fact, foods you put together without a recipe—scrambled eggs or cheese and crackers—are spells for satisfying the need we call "hunger."

So, spells don't always have to rhyme and, when they do, the rhyme doesn't have to be perfect; neither does the meter. A spell doesn't have to be Shakespearian or even grammatically correct—as many of the examples in this book demonstrate! It only has to express your intent in a way that is understandable to you, so you're able to repeat the words more than once without tripping over the cadence. But even that's not a hard-and-fast rule, because extemporaneous spells, where you may just pour your heart out explaining your need to the universe, can also work. Either way, when composing your spells, it's a good idea to be very specific about the need you're trying to meet, and less specific about the way you want to meet it. That gives the magick a wider field to work in.

WIDENING YOUR HORIZONS

If there's only one acceptable outcome for a spell, you may think there's only one way for it to come about. But you can't think of everything, so you must work your magick carefully to allow for the unexpected. Otherwise, you risk imposing on other people's free will and, sooner or later, that's going to rebound in unpleasant ways. When you think your options are limited, the spells you cast should include one to broaden your own perspective so that you can see more ways to achieve the success you desire. For example:

∞

I look up, I look down;

I look everywhere around.

Yet there are things I cannot see —

So magick, help them work for me!

When you're working to get chosen—for a job, for the team, by Ms. or Mr. Right—you want to be chosen on the basis of reality, not some befuddling spell you've cast. And remember that getting what you want is just the beginning. Keeping what you want, and continuing to want it, will take even more energy. If you've gotten it by cold trickery, you won't have that energy to spare.

FINDING THE RIGHT WORDS

If you're not sure how to find the right words for spells that you make up yourself, consider borrowing lines that have already been written, and modifying them. For example, instead of "Rain, rain, go away! Come again some other day," you could say, "Measles, measles, go away, bother me no other day."

You can also borrow familiar forms of speech, like the call-and-response technique you may have heard in other situations. "Is everybody happy?" goes the call, and "Yes!" goes the response. This may be repeated more than once. So, for example, you may say, "Am I going to get this job?" and then answer, "Yes!" more enthusiastically each of the three times you say it.

Another way is to pretend that you're a child, and phrase your spell the way you would have in your childhood. Your spell is likely to take a sing-song form, and you may even make a rocking motion while you repeat it, or walk or skip to the rhythm of the words. Including action beyond the action of speaking aloud helps raise the energy needed to power your spells. To try this technique for yourself, pick the tune to a cartoon's theme or a favorite song that's easy to sing, and make up new words to it. For a generic example, let's use the "Happy Birthday" song. If you want something you're doing to turn out well, here's what you might sing to that tune:

∞

Turn out well it will,

Turn out well it will!

I've done it just right, and

Turn out well it will!

If you want or need another verse, use this:

∞

It will make me glad,

It will make me glad!

I'm sure it will be the

Best I've ever had!

Add even more verses as you're inspired to. And if you're working on your project over a period of time, make up new songs every time you put some effort in on it. (Of course, you also have to be sure your mundane preparations are in order, and that you're paying attention and following the directions.)

Sealing Your Spells

Sealing a spell is the equivalent of dropping a letter into the mailbox or hitting send after you've signed your e-mail. There are several ways to do this, and you can use more than one per spell. Each seal should be used when the main working of the spell is done.

POWER OF THREE

∞

By the power of three times three,

As I will, so mote it be!

When using this seal, you'll want to do at least one part of the spell three times. Say it three times, write it three times, fold the paper three times, tap it three times with your fingers, turn around three times while you're holding it, or something similar.

HARM TO NONE

With harm to none

My will be done.

Many "magickal people" add a disclaimer like this to every spell they do, and you can too. Working magick is perfectly natural, and as with anything else we do, it's important that we consider its effect on other people. Just as in our mundane interactions, persuasion is fine, but coercion is not. Even when it seems to meet short-term goals, unethical behavior is neither satisfactory nor satisfying in the long run. Shady is only good when you need shelter from the UV rays of the sun.

WORK MY WILL

Into the worlds now goes my spell,

With harm to none to work my will.

This seal combines the "disclaimer" with very clear instructions for the spell to start working. Using this seal, it's easy to visualize your spell twinkling away like Tinkerbell's magick or flying away like cartoon airmail, and visualization always adds strength to a spell. Speaking of Tinkerbell, clapping your hands three times (or clicking your heels three times, if you're more of a Dorothy fan), can add a little extra oomph to any spell.

You may want to come up with your own seal, and that's fine, too.

Charmed, I'm Sure

When creating your own charm, how do you know what to put into it or, for that matter, what to use to hold the bits and pieces?

I like pouches, myself. You can make them from scraps of fabrics, or quilt squares, or buy them in the bridal section of any craft store: some are mesh-y and some are tightly woven and opaque. Either will do.

Small boxes, like the ones you can get in various shapes and inexpensively at craft stores, are also good choices, and have the advantage of being easy to decorate. If your household matches come in boxes, an empty one might be ideal.

You can use pieces of cloth gathered and tied (like a bouquet garni) or pieces of cloth sewn together (like a sachet or cushion). If what you're putting into it isn't very thick or pokey you can use an envelope of appropriate size. A shallow dish or bowl could be used, too, if you're not going to need it for anything else in the near future.

What you put in the charm will depend on what it symbolizes to you, the purpose it's meant to serve, and what you have on hand. No matter what the conventional magickal correspondences are (see the Appendices for some of them), there should be something in every charm you make that reflects your own mental and emotional connections to the purpose of your magick. You need to draw on your memories, your plans, your hopes—and everything that symbolizes them to you. If, for instance, you think that buttons represent safety, you should include a button in any charm you make for that purpose.

Brews

Most books about home remedies caution you against trying anything exotic without first checking with your doctor, or at least with your pharmacist, about any possible side-effects or interactions. This one is no different: even combining "over the counter" ingredients requires some care. If you have any doubt at all about any brew you're considering, err on the side of caution, and either check it out first or try something different.

Beyond that, your own personal preferences will have a lot to do with the ingredients you choose. Water is a common mixer for brews of any sort. Should it be hot or cold? Do you like still or sparkling water? Would you rather use tonic or soda water? Does cola settle your stomach better than another liquid?

Brews (or potions, if you like that word better) don't have to contain strange ingredients to be magickal. Anything can become magickal when you charge it with the energy of your intention. If you want a brew to be healing, you might chant a healing rhyme over it, maybe something like this:

∞

Make my throat wetter

And make me feel better.

OR

I am tired of feeling sick

And this brew will do the trick!

You can say those words over tea as it steeps, or hot cocoa as it dissolves. The cup or mug you choose may be a special one that you particularly like and you may even like to use a particular spoon or swizzle stick to stir your brews (whether they actually need stirring or not). What you choose to do is up to you! Just be sure that you have a connection to the brew you're making to enhance its magick.

Most magick we do is about getting us from one situation to another: maybe from ill to hale, from a mediocre job to a better one, or from one state of mind to another. When you look at it that way, every day of your life is a passage—at the very least, from yesterday to tomorrow. But there are some events and circumstances that we recognize as important passages, worthy of particular commemoration, and in the next chapter, we'll think about the magick we can do for some of those.

·8·

RECOGNIZING
PERSONAL
PASSAGES

We go through a great number of personal passages—births, deaths, graduations, weddings, etc.—throughout our lives. It's nice when we can share significant passages with friends, but it's not always possible. Here are some ways to mark or perhaps find the magick in your personal passages.

You'll notice that the spells in this section aren't necessarily short, and may involve a little more time, effort, or harder-to-find "ingredients" than most of the spells in this book. That's because they're about you, not just the things that happen in your life, which makes them more important than ordinary spells. The magick you work on yourself, for your emotional health and to realize your unique potential as a human being, is much more significant than the magick you do to get a parking place or avoid annoying coworkers. It's even more meaningful than the magick you do to find a life partner or find ways to mend relationships. This special magick you do to heal your soul's hurts and see yourself as the magnificent creature you really are is worth a little extra time and trouble.

Whether you work this magick in the solitary privacy of your own home or silently while you're with family, friends, or out in public, it can still be done very privately. No one else has to know. But when these spells begin to work, other people will certainly notice the changes that come over you.

Let's take a look on the following pages at some of the passages you can celebrate, always remembering that if you've passed a particular stage, you can go back and celebrate those moments or phases with your inner child!

From the Beginning

Research has made it clear that babies have the same needs that everybody else does. It's true that infants' and toddlers' and young children's needs can't be met exactly the same way that ours are, but babies need food, drink, shelter, clothing, and loving welcome into the world. Sadly, not all of us got the love we needed when we were little—but happily, it's not too late!

ROCK-A-BYE CHARM

Even adults sometimes want to be cuddled, held, or rocked for comfort. If you're fortunate enough to have grown up with loving attention, you'll remember how good it felt, and you can make a little charm to bring back those good times when you need them. If not, you can use it to give yourself the loving attention you deserved as a baby or child. You'll need:

* a cotton ball
* some baby powder
* some perfume that reminds you of your mother, grandmother, or anyone else you remember fondly from childhood
* a piece of ribbon (pink if you're female, blue if you're male) about six inches long
* a piece of cloth, white or yellow—or emphasizing those colors in its pattern if it's not solid—about five inches square or in diameter

Spread the cloth out, printed or textured side down and sprinkle it with baby powder. Put a few drops of the perfume on the cotton ball and set it in the middle of the cloth. Gather the cloth up around the cotton ball and tie it with the string. As you do this, say or sing:

∞

Rock-a-bye, baby, be safe and calm

The breath of this charm will work like a balm

Whenever I smell it, I'll know love is here

And I will be comforted, and of good cheer.

Tuck the charm away under your mattress, under the cushion of your favorite chair, or anyplace where you like to curl up and feel cozy. At every full Moon, take it out, sing the spell to it again, and add more baby powder and drops of the perfume as necessary.

FIRST DAY JITTERS

Sometimes as grownups we face situations that remind us of the first day of school: we're not sure what's going to happen or whether we'll find any friends, and we may even worry about getting lost, literally or figuratively. We may even really *be* going back to school for the first time in years. Even when it's to take classes we're sure we'll enjoy, it can make us nervous; and if the class or degree is one we need to keep or advance in our job, that can be stressful too. Here's a charm to help you deal with these situations and ease your nerves. You'll need:

* a calendar page for the month in which the first day or event occurs
* a red pen, pencil, or marker

* some gold star stickers OR a yellow marker OR a metallic gold marker
* some transparent tape

On the calendar page, draw a vibrant red circle around the date of the first "day of school." At the bottom of the page, write the date that the class, or event ends. On every day between the circled date and the last date on the calendar page, draw or stick a gold star. With your gold stars or marker, circle the ending date you've written at the bottom of the page, and draw or paste on several more gold stars around it. As you do this, say:

∞

I'm just starting out today.

I'll do well and earn my stars!

I'll learn quickly, without dismay,

Even if it's un-fa-mil-i-ar.

Time will pass and I'll soon adjust,

And my experience will be robust!

SEE YOU AFTER SCHOOL

If you are a parent and feeling a little sentimental about sending "your baby" off to school for the first time, use the following spell to ease your anxiety. Start by collecting:

* a lock of your child's hair
* a candle in the shape of the letter P (for preschool), K (for kindergarten), or the number 1 (for first grade)

* Baby powder
* a *tiny* scrap of cloth from the seam of an article of clothing that "your baby" will wear on the first day of school
* a calendar page of the month in which this event will take place
* a current photo and a baby photo are optional; if you decide to use them, I recommend making a photocopy (black and white is fine) of the two pictures, side by side, instead of using the originals
* your favorite pen
* some narrow yellow or white ribbon

Fold the calendar page in half twice, so that it's configured like a greeting card. You should be able to see at least some of the dates on the page, and if you can see the first-day-of-school date, that's super. Open the folded page as you would to read a greeting card. Sprinkle some baby powder on the paper. Say:

Once you were a baby, and now you are a child.

Place the lock of the child's hair and the scrap of seam-fabric on the baby powder, in the center of the folded segment of calendar. Say:

∞

I won't let your growing up drive me wild.

Light the P-, K-, or 1-shaped candle and let the wax drip gently onto the folded page, so that it covers the lock of hair and scrap of fabric. If you're using photos, lay those on top of the hair and the scrap of the material, and cover them with drops of wax, as well. Say:

∞

Growing up is what you're supposed to do,

So I'll rejoice and be proud of you!

I'll always be your [mom] [dad] [other caretaker] no matter what occurs

So I'll be glad your growth to spur.

Now, at the top of the segment, an inch or so away from the wax-covered spell ingredients, write "to [child's name]" and below it, toward the bottom corner of the folded segment, write, "love, [your name].

Fold the calendar-page card shut, and seal the edges with more drippings from the candle. That may not keep the folded charm closed, so tie it off with the ribbon, as if you were finishing wrapping a present. In a way, your promise to help "your baby" grow up *is* a gift, one that you're giving to your child and to yourself. You'll always cherish your child's baby days, but no one should miss out on knowing their kids as the wonderful adults they'll turn out to be. And who couldn't use a little magick to help them grow up!

CONGRATULATIONS, GRADUATE!

Our culture reminds us to celebrate when our children (or we) graduate. Sometimes you give the graduate gifts, and can give those gifts a little extra "oomph" by putting a spell on them. You're not putting a spell on the graduate by doing this, but rather are charging the *gift* with a magickal duty, so that it will help the graduate achieve his or her goals. To cast this spell, say:

∞

Gift I have chosen with love and respect,

Serve s/he who receives you so as to effect

The goals that s/he sets, the plans s/he makes,

And so that her/his dreams never fade.

Note that this spell allows your gift to "keep on giving" even if the graduate's dreams and plans change. That's much more important than precise rhymes!

Coming of Age

Commercially, coming of age is all about partying. But many parents and young adults want to recognize other qualities in more meaningful coming-of-age rites. If you're a grownup and you don't have (or plan to have) kids who will be making such a passage, you may still wish that you'd had some kind of meaningful ceremony yourself. Don't worry—remember, it's never too late! The spells that follow can charm a gift that you give to a youngster who's between the ages of twelve and fourteen, or a gift that you give to yourself to honor the coming-of-age process you had to go through alone.

NOT A KID ANYMORE

Choose a gift, and before you wrap it, hold it in both hands. Either looking at a photo of the person who will receive it, or holding their image in your mind, say:

∞

Not a child, not quite adult:

This time for her/him is difficult.

Yet full growth is the result

So her/his journey I exalt.

Now breathe on the gift, hold it to your forehead, hold it to your heart, and kiss it. After that, say:

∞

Let this gift a reminder be

That I'll be here if s/he needs me.

I'll treat her/him with respect and care

As s/he grows up with her/his own flair.

Now you can wrap the gift. Depending on the circumstances, you may like to include a card in which you write a variation of the second part of the spell, using the young person's name and saying "you" instead of s/he and him or her.

I MATTER, YOU MATTER, WE ALL MATTER

Some people remember high school as the best time of their lives. For some, however, those years were agony, which can still be felt, at least now and then. And really, who hasn't felt "like a kid again," but "in a bad way?" On those occasions, we can, for our own comfort and growth, do the occasional spell to heal that teenage hurt, lack of confidence, or poor self-image that may still be misguiding us today.

For this spell, have these items handy:

* a bottle of wine or your favorite juice
* a nice light meal (homemade or take-out, your preference)
* your high school yearbook, your graduation tassel, a photo of yourself from those days, or a drawing to represent you in those days
* copy of the following spell on a small piece of paper
* additional mementos of your high school days (optional)

Once you've gathered all of these items, follow these instructions:

1. Set your table for two. Use the nicest dinnerware and cutlery you have, and make the settings as formal as you can. Include nice wine or water glasses, and have a bottle of wine or juice ready.
2. Put on what you could call a "power outfit." This may mean dressing for an important meeting or a night out, but it might mean wearing a really great pair of jeans and a shirt that makes you look fabulous. The important thing is that you feel your best in what you're wearing.
3. Prepare a light meal to have when you're finished with the spell. Eating not only helps you ground the energy you've raised, but will also help you absorb the energy of the spell and make it part of yourself physically as well as mentally and emotionally.
4. Next, bring out your yearbook photo. If you have some other memento of those days—maybe the

tassel from your mortarboard, or a souvenir of another happy occasion—get that out as well.

5. When you have a picture of yourself and something to symbolize the happiness you found in your high school experience, take them to the table and lay them on the rim of your plate, on the side closest to the center of the table. The happy memento should be behind the picture of yourself, and you should be looking at your teen-self at the "top" of your plate.

6. Now, let the happy memento remind you of more good memories. It doesn't matter if they're big or small remembrances. Maybe you remember how your dog wagged her tail when you came home from school, no matter what mood you were in. Were your parents sympathetic? Think hard, and remember something that makes you smile.

7. Look at the picture of yourself. Acknowledge that high school was difficult for you.

8. Copy the spell onto a piece of paper so you'll have it to read. Then, pour some wine or juice into the glass at each place at your beautifully set table. Sit down in front of your plate and picture, and adjust your chair so you're comfortable.

9. Speak to that person you used to be. If you felt misunderstood, overwhelmed, or adrift then, acknowledge it now, and realize that with the magick of love, you can reach your teenaged self and give him or her what s/he needs.

10. Remember your dreams and ideals and praise them. Remember your enthusiasms and appreciate them. Remember your courage and admire it.

If you needed hugs then and didn't get them, offer them to yourself now. Visualize your teen-self and see your grown-up self walking up and embracing that youngster, embracing and seeing the best in everything s/he was. If you and your inner teenager need to cry together, that's okay. There's a napkin beside your plate. It will wipe away tears as well as spills.

11. When you and your inner teen are ready, raise your glass, and make this toast-cum-spell. Feel free to substitute your name or nickname anywhere it fits.

To my long-ago me [or, Little Your Name],
my inner teen

And all your feelings, torn between;

To all you felt and longed to feel,

I raise my glass, and guilt repeal.

My inner teen [or, Little Your Name],
you're brave and strong,

And with me always you belong.

Your energy is dear to me, and I will your protector be.

Your potential is my core. Lost at sea? Now come ashore,

And troubled or lonely be no more. By my love, your joy restore!

A NEW JOB . . . AGAIN?

Society used to expect that people would find their niche and work for the same employer, sometimes doing the same job, until they retired. Nowadays, people might go through ten or more jobs by the time they're forty! Even though the first-job thrill may be gone, the new-job jitters are still part of lots of people's lives.

Here's a spell to turn that new-job nervousness into something more creative. It is best to cast this spell on a waxing Moon, which means any time between the new Moon and a day or two before the full Moon. To cast this spell, you'll need:

* a business card or brochure from your new company; if you don't have one available, write the name, address, and other contact information on a piece of paper, and use that
* something to represent your new position at the company, so write your name and the title of the job you'll be doing on a second piece of paper
* a bowl big enough to hold the pieces of paper you've just prepared
* enough sugar to fill half the bowl you've chosen

Cover the bottom of the bowl with a layer of sugar and say the following spell over the two papers that represent your new employer and your new job.

∞

From [school][my old job] I depart,

A new job to start. A new course I chart,

And I'm plenty smart!

I'll succeed in my work; I won't go berserk.

The boss I'll impress, and I will progress

∞

With great calmness to achieve success.

With magick I infuse the work I choose.

This I avow, and no harm allow:

Success on the job begins right now!

When you've spoken the words, put the papers in the bowl and cover them with sugar. Cover the bowl, set it in the freezer, and leave it there until the Moon is full. Then, empty the sugar out of the bowl and, if you can, use it in a recipe for something you can eat within the next few hours. Burn the two pieces of paper—making sure you're doing it somewhere safe—and, as the flames consume the pieces, say:

∞

Burning up, do not disrupt.

Keep the heat in

My passion for work, so I won't shirk

And my success won't be beaten.

When you eat the goodie with the sugar, say:

∞

All success I do ingest.

You can use the same spell to charge your promotions at work with success, too. This time you'll probably be able to use your own business card. Surround it with sugar again, because you still want to keep everything about your new position "sweet." When you cast the spell, just change the last two lines to

∞

This I avow, and no harm allow:

Success in my promotion begins right now!

Whenever you do this spell, anytime in the next month that you eat anything with sugar in it, you can repeat that single line, "All success I do ingest," under your breath, to increase its potency. If the right opportunity presents itself, you could even raise a bite of dessert to those you're dining with, as if you're making a toast with it, and say, "May we all ingest . . . sweet success!"

MOVING RIGHT ALONG

Moving into a new place is exciting—and stressful! Even if you've moved before and know the ropes, there's still an awful lot to remember and attend to. If it's your first place, the whole process can be overwhelming. Here is a spell to keep yourself steady through all the work—the paper work and the actual moving.

To start, gather together:

* a *photocopy* of both sides of the signature page of your purchase or rental agreement
* one white candle

Lay out the photocopy of the purchase or rental agreement horizontally on a table or counter, with your signature toward the edge of the table, and facing you. Burn the white candle long enough for it to make some wax, and then drip a little in each of the four corners of your copy of the contract. As you do, say:

∞

New white candle, warm white wax,

Help me keep the details straight; help me to relax.

As you burn and as you dry,

Cast a spell so nothing goes awry.

Next, fold the top of the contract down about a third of the way as if you were going to put it in an envelope. As you make the crease of the fold sharp by going over it with a fingernail or the back edge of a knife, say:

∞

I am no longer status-quo-ing

Then fold the bottom half up, so that your signature is now on top (but upside down from where you're sitting or standing), and say:

∞

But I can still see what is going . . .

Turn the folded contract around so that your signature is right-side up for you, and begin to drip the wax from the white candle over your signature. Say:

∞

. . . On.

This may not make sense at first, but what you're doing is charming the photocopy of your contract with a spell to keep the rental or buying process moving along without a hitch. When you say the next part of the spell while folding the contract, you're sealing it with the wax you're dripping over your signature. You're acknowledging that things are changing—you are no longer "status quo-ing"—but at the same time you're affirming and magickally ensuring that you can cope with it. You can "still see what is going . . . on."

Whenever you're feeling overwhelmed by the whole process, just take another look at this charm, and note that you can still see your signature through the wax. Thus, metaphorically, your purpose and joy in moving is still visible through all the official (and sometimes intimidating) technicalities.

BLESS MY NEW HOME

To bless your new place, you'll need:

* a spare photo of it, which can be from an ad in the paper, a brochure, or one you've taken and printed out yourself; this should be at least four inches on the shortest side
* a new white candle
* a candle in your main decorating or favorite color
* your door key, or another key that represents your door key
* a piece of ribbon—fancy or plain—about eight inches long, and between an eighth of an inch and a half inch wide

Make this charm and cast its spell as soon as you can have some time to yourself in your new home. Set everything out on a table or a counter, and light both candles. When the white one has burned enough to make some wax that is ready to drip, hold it over the center of the picture of your home. Move the candle so the dripping wax makes a spiral (the drops can be connected, or spaced apart) of at least three loops. This spiral should turn towards the right and you should start from the inside and move out. As you form the spiral, say:

∞

New white candle, burning wick,

Let no ill-luck or malice stick.

Let all things scary, all things wrong,

From my house go, and stay gone!

You will be able to recite this spell three times, maybe more, while the candle wax drips. This spiral is carrying any and all "bad vibes" away from your house, from the center outwards, and at the same time creating a barrier so that bad vibes can't come back in.

When you have completed at least three loops of that spiral, light the colored candle. Let it drip wax in another spiral, this time moving from the outside in because you're bringing blessings into the center of your home. You can let the colored wax drip in the spaces between the loops the white wax has made. As you create the spiral with the colored wax, say:

∞

[Color] candle, dripping pale,

Hereby my magick shall avail.

May my roof ne'er fall in,

And my friends never fall out;

And may I feel at home here

As long as I'm about.

Next, add a little fresh white and colored wax to the middle, and press the house key into the warm wax. You're using the key as a seal, to confirm your intent to keep hostile influences away from your home and keep it safe and filled with grace and comfort.

Finally, roll the picture up, from right to left, and tie it with your piece of ribbon or trim. This ribbon should be long enough to make a secure knot and a bow. The knot symbolizes your determination to make your home safe, and the bow represents your intention to make it hospitable and comfortable. Don't worry if rolling the picture creases or cracks the wax drippings. Let that symbolize your home becoming well-worn with good company.

This last bit is optional: drip a little more white and colored wax over the knot in the middle of the bow, and as you do, say:

∞

*Candles flame and candle rind, ***

Leave your magick here behind.

Let this charm and spell remind

Me to keep my life in this place kind.

*"Candle rind" is a made-up term to refer to the wax you've just dripped to cast the spell.

There are two parts to working magick: the magick, and the working. When you cast this spell to "keep my life in this place kind," you're doing the magick. However, you must also be willing to do the work of being hospitable, and of caring for your house or apartment.

Relationship Magicks

When it comes to doing magick on relationships, at least relationships that involve other people, things can get tricky. Before you bless other people, much less do magick to affect your relationships with them, you have to be sure of your own motives *and* their permission. Keep this in mind as you try out the following spells.

SPELL TO BLESS A COUPLE

Almost everybody loves weddings. The optimism they represent makes them joyous, wonderful occasions. If you're the one getting married—or "civilly unioned"— you may want to bless the relationship and the new stage it's entering. For this blessing, you'll need:

* two pieces of unlined paper
* something to write with: black ink will suffice, but colored pens, markers, or crayons are more fun
* scissors
* tape
* faux jewels, silk flowers, ribbons, and other "craft" decorations (optional)

Begin by taping the two pieces of unlined paper together so that they make one piece almost two feet long. Then cut the long piece in half lengthwise, so you have two strips that are roughly four inches wide and twenty-two inches long. However, if you started with bigger paper and your strips are wider and longer, that's okay.

Now put the two pieces together, so that you can cut an even zig-zag pattern along one edge of both of them. You can cut the edges one at a time if you'd rather, but cutting them together enhances the bond between you and your partner. Next, fit one piece around your head and one around your partner's, zig-zags up. Cut them to the proper length so that when you tape them into circles, you'll each have a crown.

Don't tape them yet, though. Once they're cut to the right length, decorate them! Use your marker(s) and draw jewels or fancy designs. Decorate each one a little differently, because each of you is a distinct individual. Just make sure that the central design on each of the crown-strips, the part that will go in the center of your forehead, is the same, or at least quite similar. That represents the two of you becoming a unit, with shared ideals and goals.

When you've decorated your crowns, tape them at the back so that they'll fit. If you'd like to go and dress up a little bit for the rest of this "ritual," take a moment to do so. You might even like to get a bottle of something special ready to drink! When you're ready, exchange crowns, so that you're holding your partner's and your partner is holding yours. As you and your partner crown each other, say these words. (You can say them in unison, and crown each other at the same time, or you can do it one at a time. That's up to you.)

∞

You are the gem of my life and the beat of my heart.

My soul from yours will never part.

What the years may bring can't alter this:

Your love is my crowning bliss.

Feel free to wear your crowns for the next few minutes and again whenever you feel like it. Don't worry when eventually they fold or tear. They're only symbols of your love and, when they disintegrate, any reservoir of feeling they held will simply come home to you and your belovéd.

SPELL FOR HEALING AFTER PARTING

Sometimes, we must leave our partners, due either to choice or circumstance. Even if we "know" it's for the best, it can be heartbreaking. It's important to acknowledge strong feelings, even when we trust that they'll fade or change. Here's magick to do just that. You'll need:

* the ingredients for the following recipe
* red food coloring, OR a red pen or marker
* a baking sheet and/or several four-inch squares of aluminum foil
* white glue
* red ribbon or string 14 to 18 inches long

The first step you need to take to cast this spell is to make a batch of "Earth-friendly play dough," for which you can find a recipe at *www.teachnet.com*. Making the play dough yourself will add a little extra power to the spell, but if for any reason you'd rather not make your own, you can buy it at a craft store.

When your dough is ready, make a heart shape and put it on a baking sheet or several layers of tin foil to harden. If you decided against using food coloring in your play dough, or bought a batch of white, wait until it's dry then color it with your red marker or pen. When you and your play dough heart are both ready, hold it in both hands, slightly in front of you, and say:

∞

My heart is broken. I'm hurting now.

Literally break the heart in half. Say:

∞

I will heal, but I'm not sure how.

Hold both pieces of the dough to your heart. Say:

∞

I am sorry this had to end.

Put the pieces on the baking sheet or tin foil. Say:

∞

To honor my [love][heart], I will work to mend.

Glue the pieces back together. You'll notice that there will be some crumbs missing; there will be a hole in the dough heart, as there will be pain in yours for at least a little while. Hold the ribbon in both hands. Say:

∞

This is my trust and my memory

Of the good that was, and the good yet to be.

Tie the ribbon around the widest part of the heart, and make a nice bow. Say:

∞

With this lifeline, my heart's bedecked

And soon will be able to reconnect.

Mind you, if there's been a breakup, this doesn't mean that you'll "reconnect" with your former partner. It means you'll be able to reconnect with your social life and, in time, you'll be able to enjoy new relationships. A new relationship won't be exactly the same, but if you pay more attention to the mending than the breaking, you'll find something else that's wonderful in its own right.

TOP OF THE HILL BLESSING

As baby-boomers age there are more and more "eldering" rituals, to celebrate the wit and wisdom—and these days, continuing good health and activity—of the so-called golden years. However, you can celebrate maturity when you're as young as thirty. Turning forty, fifty, or sixty is worth celebrating too, and not just with the "over the hill" paraphernalia you can find at most party stores. Maybe there *is* a hill, but you should enjoy the hike. When you get to the top, stop to admire not only the view, but the people who've gotten there already. For this "Top of the Hill party," you'll need:

* a cake, with King _____ or Queen _____ written on it, with the name of the honoree filling in the blank
* an ordinary chair, decorated with paper flowers, streamers, or anything else you'd like
* a toy crown, which you can make or buy

Other than that, unless the guests want to bring their own gifts for the honoree, you only need to know which way is north!

When you are ready to begin, the guests need to form a circle around the honoree. Someone, probably the host of the event, should say:

[Honoree's name], today we gather to recognize your dignity,

You're a friend unlike any other, and we honor your maturity.

You're adult and responsible, but still young at heart

And thus you're extravaganzable,
and we've all come to do our part!

One person will then either lead the honored guest around the circle to each compass point, or turn him/her in place to face East, South, West, and North in turn. Say these rhymes at the appropriate direction:

"EAST"

The East has blessed you with clear sight and bright thoughts

And to all your friends, these gifts you've brought.

"SOUTH"

The South has blessed you with passion and courage

And you've shared those with all of us, your entourage

"WEST"

The West has blessed you with deep feeling and a kind heart

And with us you share the joy of friendship, and its art.

"NORTH"

The North has blessed you with reliability and pith

You're a true grownup, but still fun to play with!

Now, bring your guest back to the center. Seat him or her on the decorated chair, and gather around again. Crown your guest of honor as a king or queen, saying:

You're in control of your own life, and that we encourage,

So we crown you as a [king] [queen],
and offer you our peerage!

Sing "For S/he's a Jolly Good Fellow," and don't forget to bring out the cake when you're done. Ask the guest of honor to do the honors and cut it.

PROTECTION FOR YOUR PET

Our relationships with our companion animals are important. Fortunately, it's fine to bless them and cast a spell to make sure your relationship develops as you'd like it to, and in their best interests. For this spell you need:

* your pet's water dish, with some water in it
* a small bowl
* one of your pet's toys
* a bit of your pet's food (several bird seeds, several crushed pieces of cat or dog kibble, etc.)
* a piece of paper with your pet's name written on it, surrounded by hand-drawn hearts
* a feather or one or two strands of hair from your pet (collected after it's been naturally shed)
* a strand or two of your hair—either from your brush, or plucked especially for the occasion—cut into pieces about an inch long
* a cloth hankie, scarf, or bandana
* a photo of the animal, if it can't be in the room with you

If your pet is in the same room, it doesn't have to be paying close attention. However, you will need a work surface that the animal can't reach or can be shooed away from. If your animal can't be with you, put its photo on the counter or table.

Begin by spreading out the hankie, scarf, or bandana. It should be square to the edge of the work surface. Set the small bowl between the center and the edge of the bandana farthest away from you. Pour some of the water from your pet's water dish into the bowl. Say:

∞

By the cleansing power of rain and stream

And the quenching of thirst . . .

Add some of the animal's food to the water in the small bowl, and say:

∞

*By the nourishment of the earth and the
steadiness of its turn*

Add the strands of your hair, saying:

∞

By my love for you, through best and worst

Add the feather or fur from your animal and say:

∞

Your health and protection will always be my first concern.

Stir this "mixture" with your finger, and dab a bit of it on the pet's toy. Say:

∞

*This I promise, on my word,
for I am your only pack and herd.*

*When I cannot make things right,
I'll stay with you by day or night.*

*The shield of love is what I raise
to protect you, nights and days.*

*I won't abandon you, my dear:
that is one thing you need never fear.*

Occasions of Grief

We grieve about many things, from loss of jobs, possessions, or status to loss of life—a pet's, a friend's, our own. Grief is a normal feeling when something meaningful is lost, and it's not unworthy or unhealthy to mourn for our losses. However, it's only when we acknowledge our griefs and work through them that we can move beyond our pain and restore joy to our lives. There is no magick to eliminate loss or sorrow from our lives—nor should there be, as that's part of what makes us human—but there is magick we can do to help ourselves through the rough patches.

SPINNING SADNESS

When we face situations that could result in significant loss—a round of layoffs at work that could leave us jobless, or a tumor that may be malignant—we often experience anticipatory grief. We understand that our lives may be about to change drastically, and we begin to imagine what it will be like to give up what we have now. But, realistically, there's a chance that we *won't* lose our job or that the tumor will be benign. Even if worse comes to worst, it's likely that we'll have the support of our friends, or other alternatives that we haven't even imagined. The truth is that change is constant, and what's really nerve-wracking is the feeling that we can't *control* the changes in our lives.

This spell will help put all of that in perspective, and let you focus on the power you *do* have. The name of this spell alludes to the way grief can make us dizzy, and the way we can "spin" our uncomfortable energies into something more constructive. For this spell, you'll need:

* a piece of paper at least three inches by five inches
* a pen or pencil

On the paper, in big letters that leave only about a half-inch margin around the word, write SADNESS. Now think of two or three words that describe your anxiety. If you're wondering whether you're going to be one of the people laid off at your company, your three words could be "unemployment," "repossession," and "homelessness." Write the scariest of these words inside the D of SAD-NESS, and the other two along the stems of the N.

In the margins you've left around the word SAD-NESS, write the names of friends and family members who could help. Could Joe on the bowling team let you crash in his spare room if you needed to? Does Judy from church know of someone who has an apartment to rent? Will Cousin Stacy invite you to dinner once a week? Did that clerk at the grocery store mention something about an opening at her brother-in-law's firm? Do *you* know of some opportunities that haven't been worth exploring until now? Write a few words in the margins that refer to all of these strands in your support net.

Now fold each end of the card in toward the center, so that it looks like double doors are opening onto the word SADNESS. Say:

∞

I'm feeling sad now, this is true,

And I have good reason to.

But I have several options, too.

If worst should happen, at least I do

Have some ways of coming through.

Bend the folds of the cards back and forth, as though you're opening and closing the doors. Say:

∞

One door may close, but another will open;

If one chance leaves, another will beckon.

The doom that threatens isn't iron-clad

And I begin to close the doors on being sad.

SPINNING WORRY

If your concerns are with health issues, here's another spell to cast on yourself. It won't guarantee that things will turn out the way you want them to, but it will help you cope with whatever does happen. Again, all you need is a piece of paper and a pen or pencil.

In the center of the paper, leaving wide margins at the side and narrow margins at the top and bottom, draw a stick figure—or a more realistic representation if you're so inclined—of yourself, with an emphasis on the part of your body that is ailing. Do the same thing on the other side of the paper, leaving the same margins. On one side, give your stick figure a frowny face. On the other side of the paper, give your stick figure a smiley face. If someone else's health is worrying you, draw a picture of yourself and add a thought-bubble with that person's initials in it. Remember, you must *never* work magick on or for another person without their explicit permission. Now fold one of the wide side margins over so it covers the unhappy figure, and fold the other so it covers the happy figure. Hold the accordion-folded paper in your hands, and press the folded edge over the unhappy figure, saying:

༚

I'm closing the door on sadness and pain

And on any worsening of my days . . .

Now open the fold on the other side, so the happy figure is visible again, and say:

༚

And open the door to hope I can regain

And every sign of health embrace.

Keep this charm handy, and feel free to close the door on the unhappy figure and open it for the happy one whenever you need a reminder that life still has gifts for you and you can still enjoy them even if you can't control what ails you.

SPINNING ANGER

Again, it's normal to feel grief and anger when we have to endure big, unpleasant changes. You're allowed to vent your rage and fear. Sometimes you just need to howl it out, and that's fine! Here's another spell to spin with. All you need for this spell is your own supply of satisfying expletives, and an appropriately private environment in which to expel them. Feel free to literally spin while casting this spell. While spinning, say:

∽

I am angry, angry, angry

That [a short description of your affliction] has befallen

And I am scared, scared, scared

And I've a right to be crestfallen.

I've suffered a blow, but all will again be well —

Just not until a few expletives I yell!

SPINNING THE WHINE

As you fall asleep each night, recapping three things that lifted your spirits during the day is a great way to count your blessings and send you off to peaceful slumber. They don't have to be grand or elegant things. It'd be great to have this list:

1. won the Nobel prize
2. won the lottery
3. saw the headlines about world peace finally breaking out

But most people's lists are more like

1. the dryer didn't rip holes in anything
2. the cat rubbed on me and purred
3. there was enough bread to make a sandwich for lunch

That's fine. The secret to life is the celebration of all its gifts. If your list is about not getting a headache, having a perfectly steeped cup of tea, and remembering a great day ten years ago, then those are the gifts you unwrapped and enjoyed. They should be precious.

When illness or circumstance confines us to a smaller world, we may need to look more carefully for the reflections of the sun and stars and the gifts that we receive daily. This spell will help your eyes adjust when the light changes.

∞

I won't waste energy bemoaning

My unexpected fate.

My attention I'll be honing

And turn to what's to celebrate.

Celebrating Accomplishments

Everyone faces losses, but everyone also has accomplishments to celebrate. Here are spells and charms to help you do that. When you do these spells, have on hand:

* a bottle of champagne or a package of confetti
* a tube of glitter (optional)

You can use these spells to charm the champagne you drink or the confetti you toss (perhaps at your image in the mirror). You can also use these spells to charm a tube of glitter, and when you need a little extra boost in your endeavors, you can put a pinch of that shiny success magick in your shoe or in your pocket. No one else will see it, but it will help you achieve another victory. These spells will let you drink in your success, and realize that your accomplishment is really something to celebrate. Congratulations, by the way!

If you are congratulating someone else, change the pronouns to fit, and use the rhymes as toasts rather than spells. The difference is that when you toast someone, they have the option to accept or refuse the blessing, whereas when you put a spell on someone else, you are leaving them no immediate choice.

RAH-RAH SPELL

∞

Way to go, Me! Job well done,

I worked real hard for this reward

And now I am a cham-pi-on!

May future success around this one coalesce!

ATTA-BOY SPELL

∞

I wasn't sure that I could, but I did.

And now of self-doubt I can be rid.

My confidence is higher; I'm a never-say-dier

And a success intensifier!

Final Blessings

No matter our cultural differences and the fact that our personal styles are almost infinitely varied, we all come of age, attain maturity, become elders, and eventually pass from this world. And everyone needs occasional help finding their way through these seasons of life. Wiccan tradition tends to associate the seasons of life with the four cardinal directions—East, South, West, and North—and the cycle of life with Spirit. This book ends with six blessings that honor this tradition. They can be self-blessings or, with permission, you can bestow them on others. I've saved them for last because they represent the life cycle, coming full circle, and the ultimate realization that each of us truly *is* a magickal being. They also summarize the symbolism and perspectives that have guided me in writing this book, and that I hope will encourage and empower your own use of magick.

COMING OF AGE

East is the direction of beginnings, so I offer a blessing of East for coming of age. It's never too late.

∞

See a whole life's dawns before you,
and take blessing from the East:

With joy and hope and energy, go upon your Quest in peace.

GREAT GROWNUP

South represents the prime of life, so I bring a blessing of the South to maturity.

∞

Feel the heart of fire above you,
and take blessing from the South:

Stand fast with those who love you.
Quest for passion and the truth.

ELDERHOOD

West represents empathy and a oneness with life, the universe, and everything else, so I give you a blessing of the West for elderhood.

∞

Hold the beauty of the sunset
and take blessing from the West:

In wisdom and without regret let faith sustain your Quest.

FAREWELL

North represents the Earth, the mystery of the Mother who is both womb and grave, so I have composed a blessing of North for parting and requiem.

∞

Accept the comfort of the evening
and take blessing from the North:

Fear you not the brief'ning but rest; and then once more set forth.

THE QUEST CONTINUES

Spirit is all-encompassing, the center that permeates everything, so I present a blessing of Spirit for seekers of guidance.

∞

Be still within the center and by Spirit now be blessed:

To your true will but surrender and your path will manifest.

SIXTH BLESSING

The sixth blessing is from me to you, with my thanks for your attention to this book, to the spells, charms, and brews, and my cautions.

∞

May you never fear your power.
May your spirit e'er be strong.

May you always feel the wonder, and know that you belong.

Bright blessings and success in all your proper quick and simple spells!

AFTERWORD

With so many movies and television shows emphasizing the supernatural these days, it's easy to think that magick is all about wizards and witches aiming shock waves of energy here and there, or that it's all about puffs of smoke and hunching over some vile-smelling vat that boils ominously. As a fully ordained Wiccan minister, I see magick in places where other people see coincidence or synchronicity, courtesy, luck, strategy, determination, unexpected beauty, etc. The truth is that lots of people do magick every day, most of them without even knowing it.

When you take a deep breath and set your shoulders before going into an important meeting, that's a spell: it has intention and power behind it. When you hold the elevator door for someone, or let someone with one or two items go through the check stand ahead of you and your full cart, that's a blessing from their perspective and an intentional act of kindness on yours: in other words, it is an exchange of energy that achieves the goal of making the world a better place. Over time and with experience, I've learned to see that as magick. I hope this book has helped you redefine the concept, too.

When we choose to see the world as magickal, we allow ourselves to see more possibilities. When we see more possibilities, we can feel less threatened. When we feel less threatened, we can act less defensively. And when we act less defensively, we have more energy and attention available to appreciate each other and all those possibilities for joy and fulfillment.

This is why I've written this book. I know there will be some in my religious community who call it superficial, and some who will say that I'm sharing too much, "enabling" readers to go nuts and use magick irresponsibly, and that any mistakes you make will be on my head. But I'm not worried. I trust you. You and I both know that what we do in the world matters, and how we do it matters too. I'm not taking any bigger risk in sharing these charms, chants, brews, and magicks with you than the risks your driving instructor or math teacher took.

It's also my strong belief that, across the board, the more aware we are of what we're doing, the more effective we're going to be. I offer these spells as tools to boost your awareness of the power you have in your own life. These spells are meant to empower you to be the leading actor in your own life, not the controlling demagogue in anyone else's. Being comfortable with your own authority is a basic human right. That doesn't mean any of us is an island—none of us are. We're a cooperative species, but to cooperate we have to be able to operate in the first place.

We all have somewhere that we need to go. My car is a stick-shift, and while I may occasionally "take the scenic route" to get somewhere, I decide for myself when it's time to change gears. That's what this book is really about: giving you the power to shift your own life to get where you want to go—without running over anybody else on the way.

APPENDIX A

Flavor Correspondences

This list sets forth some of the goals you can work toward with various flavors. Some are traditional folk remedies of physical ailments, but before using them as such, be sure to check with your doctor. Other flavors correspond with magickal "powers." Any flavor you really like can be charged with the following spell to work for any honorable purpose. Just fill in the blank appropriately and say:

> *Favorite flavor, I instill*
> *You with the power to do my will.*
> *My goal is _____, and when I taste*
> *You, with success I will be graced.*
> *With harm to none, this work be done!*

Blackberry: magickally said to encourage favorable outcomes

Cherry: remedially soothing to a sore throat and, by extension, magickally good for making it easier to speak publicly or to individuals; it's also associated with knowledge and seeing through deception

Chocolate: often curative of headaches, it's well known as a pick-me-up; magickally, it can inspire reverence and/or inspiration

Coffee: remedially it can be a diuretic; magickally it encourages concentration, follow-through, and prosperity

Lemon: magickally associated with raising energy and improving stick-to-it-iveness

Lime: magickally helpful in making yourself attractive or receptive to romantic love

Orange: magickally reinforces sincerity and generosity; associated with all things bridal

Peppermint: remedially it's good for headache, stomach upsets, menstrual cramps, and as a pick-me-up; magickally it's associated with friendship

Raspberry: remedially soothing of coughs, colds, and morning sickness; magickally useful in working through remorse or regret

Strawberry: magickally it reinforces self-esteem and appreciation of others and enhances love of all kinds

Vanilla: magickally associated with freshness in the sense of turning over a new leaf or making a new beginning, and with romance

APPENDIX B

Color Associations

Some of these associations are based on or extrapolated from chakra-lore (chakras being the body's energy centers). Use them as guidelines, but defer to any very strong meanings that colors have for you. You may prefer one shade of a particular color to another, too, and that's fine. After all, you can magickally combine colors with a little less inhibition than you may use when painting your house!

Black: serenity OR distress, depending on personal experience and circumstances

Blue: spirit and spirituality; religious belief

Blue-green: emotions, care-taking, and responsibility for others

Brown: stillness, strength

Green: the natural world and processes

Grey: neutrality; understanding without judgment

Indigo: peace—inner, world, or regional

Orange: balance of all kinds, mental, physical, and emotional

Red: life energy, from primal and unconscious to self-aware delight in being alive; healing and the will to live

Violet: magick and transcendence

White: fullness, contentment, competence

Yellow: intellect, discernment, imagination, play

Letter Correspondences

These correspondences are based partly on traditional understanding and partly on modern cultural meanings. They are listed here as guidelines. If particular letters have very strong associations in your mind, use those instead.

A first rate, top-notch, primo; mobility; wealth

B second fiddle but not without merit; industriousness; removal of undesired things; interior activity

C contentment; comfort

D inner strength; creativity

E self-protection; inner spirit; peace; regeneration

F generosity; foundations (of buildings and character, not charitable or other institutions)

G honor; dignity; groundedness

H flexibility; sensuality; universal life

I cold clarity; despair; resignation

J soul; inner resources

K inner light; curiosity; protection

L depth; protection; divination

M brotherhood; leadership; synthesis

N need; rebirth; expansion

O the sun; abundance; eloquence; survival

P humor; bravado; immortality

Q mystery; respect; awe

R distance; change; independence

S guidance; adaptability; immunity

T boldness; sympathy; perfection; justice

U pride; conviction; organization; inner work

V victory; righteousness; peace

W joy; liberty; appreciation of life's finer aspects

X gifts; blessedness; fate

Y plenty; order; justice

Z willing sacrifice; ruthlessness; relationships

APPENDIX D

Letters and their Numerical Meanings

When calculating the numerical value of your name, add the numbers, then add the two (or more) digits of the total. For example, the name *Ann* has a preliminary value of 11, because A = 1 and each N = 5, and 1 + 5 + 5 = 11. Now you must add the ones together: 1 + 1 = 2, so the final value of the name *Ann* is 2. The name *Katie* works out to 2 + 1 + 2 + 9 + 5 = 19. When you add the one and the nine, you get 10—which is still a two-digit number. In this case, add the 1 and the 0, to get a final value of 1.

A 1		**E** 5		**I** 9		**M** 4		**Q** 8		**U** 3		**Y** 7
B 2		**F** 6		**J** 1		**N** 5		**R** 9		**V** 4		**Z** 8
C 3		**G** 7		**K** 2		**O** 6		**S** 1		**W** 5		
D 4		**H** 8		**L** 3		**P** 7		**T** 2		**X** 6		

1 You seek to understand the root causes of the events of your life; analysis may be one of your strong points and you may sometimes overthink things.

2 You are concerned with balance. You are probably level-headed and able to see all sides of a situation, but may need to improve at decision-making.

3 You are good at synthesis and reconciliation. You may have—or need to discover—leadership skills; you may be innovative.

4 You are concerned with stability, and like a clear distinction between "inner" and "outer." You can see the value of working slowly and surely toward a goal, and may need to allow yourself a little more spontaneity.

5 You tend to see things in terms of challenge—or struggle. This can lead you to keep things in perspective, or to isolate yourself unnecessarily.

6 You are interested in expanding horizons. You are curious, open minded, and unafraid; recklessness could be a problem.

7 You are inclined to "inner work." You can be very honest with yourself—and it can be hard for you to accept the support of your friends and family.

8 You are often motivated by inspiration. You may need to learn that you don't always have to wait for inspiration: sometimes you need to "just do it."

9 You appreciate completion, whether in tasks or relationships. You won't abandon projects or commitments, but need to remember that "completion" doesn't necessarily mean "ending."

APPENDIX E

Gifts for Anniversaries

Anniversary	Traditional	Modern	Anniversary	Traditional	Modern
1st	paper	clocks	10th	aluminum	diamond
2nd	cotton	china	15th	crystal	watches
3rd	leather	crystal	20th	china	platinum
4th	flowers	appliances	25th	silver	silver
5th	wood	silverware	30th	pearl	diamond
6th	iron	wood	35th	coral	jade
7th	wool	desk sets	40th	ruby	ruby
8th	bronze	linen	45th	sapphire	sapphire
9th	pottery	leather	50th	gold	gold

Bibliography

Cunningham, Scott and David Harrington. *The Magical Household.* (St. Paul, MN: Llewellyn, 1980)

Frey, Diane. *The Infinite Mind.* (LCM Productions, broadcast on public radio stations the week of October 25, 2000)

Goodwin, Fred. *The Infinite Mind.* (LCM Productions, broadcast on public radio stations the week of October 25, 2000)

Greenaway, Kate. *The Language of Flowers.* (New York, NY: Gramercy Publishing, 2002)

Happy Anniversary.com: *www.happy-anniversary.com*

LaRoche, Loretta. "The Joy of Stress." (Boston, MA: WGBH, 1995)

Margo's Magical Letter Page: *www.trismegistos.com/MagicalLetterPage/Mystics.html*

About.com: Marriage: *www.marriage.about.com*

Potts, Billie. *Witches Heal.* (Ann Arbor, MI: DuRêve Publications, 1988)

Starhawk. *The Spiral Dance.* (San Francisco, CA: HarperSanFrancisco, 1989)

Sutton-Smith, Brian. *The Ambiguity of Play* (Boston, MA: Harvard University Press, 2001)

ABOUT THE AUTHOR

Ashleen O'Gaea is a Third Degree Wiccan priestess, ordained by the internationally recognized and respected Aquarian Tabernacle Church. She is the author of *Raising Witches: Teaching the Wiccan Faith to Children*; *Celebrating the Seasons of Life: Samhain to Ostara,* and *Beltane to Mabon*; and *Family Wicca: Practical Paganism for Parents and Children*. O'Gaea lives with the love of her life in Tucson, Arizona, where she has long been active in the Neo-Pagan community. When she's not at her desk, she's likely to be camping, petting a cat, or enjoying the sunset from her patio.

Contact her at:
P.O. Box 35962
Tucson, Arizona 85704-5962